SHOW UP
FOR LIFE

A Personal Road Map for Navigating the Journey

Alonzo Johnson, Ph.D.

ASYS Press

OASYS Press ◊ McDonough, GA
SHOW UP for Life:
A Personal Road Map for Navigating the Journey

Copyright © 2026 by OASYS Press. All rights reserved. No part of this book may be reproduced or transmitted in any form or by any means, electronic or mechanical, including photocopying, recording or by any information storage and retrieval system, without written permission from the author, except for the inclusion of brief quotations in a review.

This book provides information about personal development. It is sold with the understanding that the publisher and author make no representations or warranty with respect to the accuracy or completeness of the content contained herein, and disclaim any implied warranties of merchantability or fitness for a particular purpose. The content of this book may not be suitable for your situation. If you require expert assistance, seek the services of a competent professional. The author and publisher shall have neither liability nor responsibility to any person or entity with respect to any loss or damage caused, or alleged to have been caused, directly or indirectly, by the information contained in this book.

Printed in the United States of America

First Edition, 2026

Visit the author's website:

www.CoachAlonzo.com

ISBN:
Print: 978-0-9863965-8-8
e-book: 978-0-9863965-9-5

◊ ◊ ◊ ◊ ◊

SHOW UP for Life is available for sale at special quantity discounts. For more information, please visit CoachAlonzo.com or email inquiries to Info@CoachAlonzo.com.

What others are saying about this book:

"In *SHOW UP for Life*, Alonzo provides a refreshing and insightful guide to actively participating in and shaping your life's path. Whether you're facing a pivotal decision or seeking to infuse more intention into your daily life, this book offers the wisdom and tools you need to take meaningful steps forward. *SHOW UP for Life* reflects Alonzo's gift for guiding others with clarity, heart, and purpose. Practical, uplifting, and rooted in real-world experience, this book is a powerful reminder that true success starts with how we show up — for ourselves and each other."

— Paula Kommor
Chief Energizing Officer, NBHWC, ACC, MEd, CPA
Dynamic Wellness — Stress Management for Professionals

"*SHOW UP For Life* is exactly what it purports to be, a road map for navigating life's journey! Coach Alonzo uses SHOW UP as an acronym to present insights and actionable steps to equip readers with tools to confidently navigate life's challenges and create a life of purpose and fulfillment. Having worked with Alonzo on several projects over the years, I can tell you that this book is a culmination of his years of coaching and mentoring experience. It is a powerful guide for anyone ready to embrace intentional living and build the life they love. This book is a must-read for anyone searching for purpose on life's journey."

— Thomas W. Norris, ACC, MEd
TRUE NORTH Coaching Solutions

"*SHOW UP For life* isn't just another book; it's a playbook for real life! If you have ever wondered how to figure yourself out or how to bounce back when life gets tough or even how to maintain your motivation, this book is for you. Using the acronym SHOW UP, Coach Alonzo guides readers through a journey of self-discovery and growth, offering practical advice and relatable anecdotes from his own experience. The book is truly a road map, which provides tips on facing challenges with confidence, taking care of yourself and celebrating life's journey as much as the destination. This book is next level, and a useful guide to help you find your purpose!"

— Georgi Aguirre
Educator/Literacy Specialist, Illinois Schools

"In *SHOW UP For Life,* Dr. Johnson invites you on a journey of intentional living—where showing up isn't just about presence, but about purpose, impact, and authenticity. With a powerful blend of insight and inspiration, Dr. Johnson challenges us to move beyond passive ambition and embrace a life of fulfillment rooted in self-awareness and meaningful connection.

Whether you're a seasoned professional, navigating mid-career transitions, or just beginning your journey, this book offers a roadmap to elevate both your personal and professional life. Dr. Johnson doesn't just speak to your goals—he speaks to your soul, urging you to align with purpose over passion and to choose a path that resonates deeply with who you are."

— Davis M. Robinson, PhD, SHRM-CP
Owner, Horizon Consulting Services, LLC

Contents

Acknowledgements	1
Preface	2
Introduction	4

Part I: Be Self-Aware — 8

1: Understanding Self-Awareness	9
2: The Importance Of Self-Reflection	24
3: Identifying Your Strengths And Weaknesses	40
4: Emotional Intelligence	54
5: Mindfulness And Present-Moment Awareness	73

Part II: Have A Sense Of Humor — 84

6: The Power Of Laughter	85
7: Humor In Social Interactions	96
8: Humor In The Workplace	108
9: Overcoming Challenges With Humor	117

Part III: Be Optimistic — 125

10: Understanding Optimism	126
11: Developing An Optimistic Attitude	141
12: Optimism In Action	153
13: Influencing Others With Optimism	162

Part IV: Show Warmth — 172

14: The Importance Of Warmth	173

15: Developing Warmth	183
16: Warmth In Everyday Interactions	196
17: Overcoming Barriers To Warmth	205

Part V: Be Unselfish — 219

18: Understanding Unselfishness	220
19: Practicing Generosity	230
20: Collaborative Mindset	238
21: Balancing Selflessness And Self-Care	251

Part VI: Find Purpose — 262

22: The Importance Of Purpose	263
23: Creating A Vision	277
24: Inspiring Others With Your Purpose	288
Conclusion: Following The Show Up Road Map	301
Suggested Readings	310
About The Author	313

ACKNOWLEDGEMENTS

No one shows up for life alone. My deepest gratitude goes to the community of incredible people who showed up for me, making this book a reality.

To my editor, Beth Kimani Davis, thank you for your vision and unwavering belief in this project. Your guidance transformed my scattered thoughts into a cohesive message.

To my early manuscript readers—especially Jeffrey Corkran, Frances Johnson Paschall, Kimberlea D. Johnson and Joel D. Weeks—thank you for spending countless hours reading, and helping to organize this book. Your willingness to provide honest feedback helped refine these ideas into something that I hope will be truly helpful to others.

To my friends, and family who took the time to read the book at various stages and provide valuable feedback, this book would not have been possible without you—a heartfelt thank you!

Finally, and most importantly, to you, the reader. You showed up here, seeking your own path forward, and I am humbled and grateful that you chose to bring this book along for the journey. My deepest thanks for inviting my words into your life. Your courage to show up for yourself is my ultimate inspiration.

PREFACE

It's common to have days when it feels easier to avoid participating and engaging in life, allowing it to happen to you rather than for you. This might present itself as a subtle feeling, a sense of not reaching your full potential, or a strong feeling of emptiness. If this feeling of wanting more but not knowing how to achieve it resonates, then this book is for you.

SHOW UP For Life is an invitation and a call to action to face life with courage and authenticity, embracing both challenges and successes. This book calls for you to consciously engage in the present moment, choosing presence over passivity, and actively building a desired life. It serves as a promise that by choosing to "show up," you will unlock a deeper sense of purpose, connection, and fulfillment.

Real change begins when a person makes the decision to fully participate in their life, regardless of circumstances. This book will give you insights, strategies, and reflections to help you navigate the path to a more engaged and meaningful existence.

To do this, you'll find tools to cultivate self-awareness, practice mindfulness, build resilience, and connect with others on a deeper level. You'll be encouraged to explore your values, identify your passions, and create a roadmap for a life that aligns with your true self.

This book draws on many years of experience that I've gained from coaching leaders across the globe. Many of these leaders used the concepts covered in this book to SHOW UP and find purpose in their own lives. I hope that this book will serve as a road map to inspire, guide, and empower you to SHOW UP as well.

INTRODUCTION

From endless notifications and back-to-back meetings to social unrest, economic uncertainty, and a constant stream of headlines that make you question where society is headed, our world today is loud, fast-paced, and often overwhelming. Understandably so, it's easy to feel like we're just trying to keep up.

But in the midst of all this chaos, there's one principle that can give us some form of stability, ground us, empower us, and transform our lives—showing up.

But what does it really mean to show up?

"This is making a conscious decision to show up both physically and mentally to engage with our surroundings and the people in it, to be present in the moment, and to commit ourselves to our goals and relationships."

From personal experience, I can tell you that showing up consistently has been a game-changer. But it's not just about being there; it's about being present with intention and purpose. Whether you're aiming for a promotion at work, building stronger relationships with loved ones, or simply striving for personal growth, showing up is the first step towards achieving those goals.

I wrote **"SHOW UP For Life: A Personal Road Map for Navigating the Journey"** to serve as a guide to understanding the importance of this principle and how it can lead you to success.

SHOW UP, in this context, is an acronym touching on six foundational aspects of life, providing you with a comprehensive roadmap on how to show up effectively:

- Be **S**elf-aware
- Have a sense of **H**umor
- Be **O**ptimistic
- Show **W**armth
- Be **U**nselfish
- Find **P**urpose

Let's take a quick tour through what you'll find in each aspect:

Part I: Be Self-Aware

We'll kick things off by taking a thorough look into self-awareness. Understanding yourself—your strengths, weaknesses, motives, and reactions—is crucial for any journey of self-improvement. Through chapters on self-reflection techniques, journaling, SWOT analysis, emotional intelligence, and mindfulness, you'll understand how you can become more aware of who you are.

This section also includes worksheets and personal anecdotes designed to help you assess and enhance your level of self-awareness.

Part II: Have a Sense of Humor

In Part II, we will explore another key ingredient for success—humor. Laughter can diffuse tension, foster connections, and even improve mental health. We'll examine scientific studies on the benefits of humor and provide strategies for incorporating humor into your daily interactions. Whether it's using humor at work or overcoming challenges with laughter, you'll discover how a sense of humor can be a powerful tool in your life.

Part III: Be Optimistic

Having an optimistic outlook can significantly impact your ability to achieve success. By understanding the differences between optimism and pessimism and learning various techniques, such as gratitude practice and visualization, you'll be better equipped to maintain a positive attitude even in the face of adversity. We will also touch on real-life examples from figures like J.K. Rowling and Malala Yousafzai to inspire you to embrace optimism in your own journey.

Part IV: Show Warmth

Warmth goes hand-in-hand with empathy and kindness—it's about creating genuine connections through sincere gestures. This part focuses on how warmth can strengthen relationships both personally and professionally. You'll learn active listening skills, ways to cultivate empathy, and techniques for creating welcoming environments.

Part V: Be Unselfish

Unselfishness is about prioritizing others while balancing your own needs. We'll examine behaviors that exemplify unselfishness and offer practical advice on practicing generosity through volunteering or supporting causes you care about. Important, too, is knowing how to balance selflessness with self-care—avoiding burnout while setting boundaries.

Part VI: Find Purpose

The final part of this book centers around finding and living your purpose. Understanding why you get out of bed each day can provide immense clarity and motivation. We'll guide you through identifying your passions, creating a personal mission statement, setting purpose-driven goals, and making sure these align with your actions.

Throughout ***"SHOW UP For Life,"*** I've included stories from my own experiences as well as those from others who've successfully navigated their journeys by showing up for themselves and others. By the end of this book, you'll have a set of actionable strategies tailored specifically for fostering self-awareness, humor, optimism, warmth, unselfishness, and, ultimately, discovering a powerful sense of purpose in your life's voyage.

Ready?

PART I
BE SELF-AWARE

1

UNDERSTANDING SELF-AWARENESS

"Knowing yourself is the beginning of all wisdom."

~Aristotle

Have you ever taken a step back—right after a certain action or, even more powerfully, just before—to ask yourself, *"Why did I react the way I did?"* or *"Why do I feel compelled to act this way?"* When we can step back and view our actions, emotions, and even thoughts from a bird's-eye perspective, this is when we begin to access true self-awareness.

In simple terms, self-awareness is the ability to see yourself clearly and objectively through reflection and introspection. It's like having a mental mirror that lets you understand your thoughts, emotions, and actions. This involves not just recognizing them but also understanding why you think or feel a certain way and how it influences your behavior.

Think of self-awareness as getting to know the real you, beneath all the layers of external influences and social conditioning. When we understand ourselves better, we can make more informed choices and live more authentically. Self-awareness also influences how we interact with people around us, making relationships stronger and more meaningful.

When I first started working on my self-awareness, it wasn't always comfortable to face my flaws and insecurities. But it was eye-opening nonetheless. For example, I used to get really defensive when given feedback at work or home. As I became more self-aware, I learned to take a step back and consider why I felt attacked or why I was reacting so strongly.

At this point, we have a general idea of why self-awareness is so essential, but let's dive into the benefits in detail:

1. **Improved Emotional Intelligence:** Self-awareness is a fundamental component of emotional intelligence. When you understand your emotions, you can manage them more effectively rather than being controlled by them. Let's say you usually get angry or frustrated when things don't go your way; if you're self-aware, you can pinpoint the root cause of this anger and address it constructively rather than lashing out.

2. **Better Decision-Making:** Knowing yourself helps you make decisions that align with your true values and goals. When you're faced with choices— whether they're as big as career changes or as small as daily habits—understanding what truly makes you happy or fulfilled can guide these decisions more effectively.

3. **Enhanced Relationships:** When you're in tune with your own thoughts and feelings, you become more adept at understanding others as well. With self-awareness, empathy

comes naturally because you can relate to people's experiences by reflecting on your own.

4. **Personal Growth:** Being aware of your strengths and weaknesses is the foundation of personal development. It helps you identify areas that require improvement, pinpoint skills that need honing, and where you excel the most.

When we begin our journey toward self-awareness, one of the most important things we can do is be compassionate with ourselves. This isn't a time for harsh self-criticism or judgment. Consider how you'd support a friend going through a similar experience. You'd probably offer them your support, patience, and loads of encouragement—offer yourself the same.

Now, you might wonder how we measure self-awareness, as it seems quite intangible. It's not like stepping on a scale to measure weight loss! However, it is still doable, and one way is through feedback from others—peers, family members, or mentors—who can offer perspectives different from our own. Additionally, personal reflection through journaling can reveal patterns in thoughts and behaviors that might not always be obvious in the moment.

The aim here isn't perfection but progress; small steps add up over time to create significant changes. So, take moments regularly to check in with yourself— *how are you feeling? Why do you think that is? What can you learn from this experience?*

As we gain a deeper understanding of ourselves, we not only enrich our personal lives but also become better equipped to handle the complexities of human interactions more effectively.

TECHNIQUES TO ENHANCE SELF-AWARENESS IN DAILY LIFE

Self-awareness isn't something we achieve once and check off a list—it's a daily practice and a skill we strengthen over time. Think of it as an internal compass that helps us navigate through life, understanding our thoughts, emotions, and actions.

Let's look at some practical techniques to boost our self-awareness and live a more mindful life.

1. Journaling

One of the most effective ways to increase self-awareness is through journaling. Every day, take a few minutes to jot down your thoughts and feelings. Write about what happened during the day, how you reacted to different situations, and why you think you acted that way. Over time, you'll start spotting patterns in your behavior and emotions.

Example Journal Entry Template

Date: _____

Mood: _____

Today's Event: (Describe a significant event)

How I Felt: _____

Why I Think I Felt That Way: _____

What I Learned About Myself: _____

2. Mindfulness Meditation

Mindfulness meditation is a fantastic technique for enhancing self-awareness. It involves focusing on the present moment, and acknowledging your thoughts and feelings without judgment.

Try this: Set aside 5-10 minutes each day to sit quietly and focus on your breath. When your mind wanders—and it will—gently bring it back to the breath. This gentle returning—over and over again—is where the self-awareness grows.

3. Seek Feedback from Others

Sometimes, we can't see ourselves clearly because we're too close to the situation. This is where feedback from trusted friends, family members, or colleagues comes in handy. Ask them how they perceive you in various situations. Their feedback can help you understand how your behavior affects others and offer new perspectives on your actions.

4. Practice Self-Reflection

Set aside some quiet time at the end of each day to reflect on the events that took place. Ask yourself questions like:

- What went well today?
- What didn't go as planned?
- How did I react emotionally?
- What could I have done differently?

This kind of self-reflection helps you identify areas for improvement and celebrate small victories.

5. Monitor Your Self-Talk

The thoughts we have in our minds can significantly influence our behavior and attitudes. Pay attention to your inner dialogue—if it's negative or overly critical, work on shifting it toward a more positive and supportive tone.

6. Set Personal Boundaries

Understanding where you want to draw the line with others helps enhance self-awareness about what feels right or wrong for you personally. Boundaries indicate comfort zones, and respecting them fosters self-respect.

7. Emotional Regulation Techniques

Developing techniques for managing your emotions is crucial for improving self-awareness. Some strategies include:

- Deep Breathing Exercises
- Counting backward from ten
- Engaging in physical activity—like walking or yoga

These methods can help calm your mind when emotions run high, allowing clearer thinking.

8. Celebrate Your Strengths & Acknowledge Weaknesses

Take note of what you're good at as well as areas where there's room for improvement. Recognizing these aspects contributes significantly towards authentic self-appreciation and growth.

For instance:

STRENGTHS	WEAKNESSES
Good listener	Procrastinates
Empathetic	Struggles with time-management
Creative thinker	Avoids confrontation

Recognize that both strengths and weaknesses form the complete picture of who we are.

Keep in mind that we've just skimmed the surface here! We'll dive deeper into these techniques in later chapters, discussing how to apply them effectively in various aspects of life.

SELF-AWARENESS IN ACTION
My Turning Point at Work

There's one particular moment in my career that really brought self-awareness to the forefront. At the time, I was working for a consumer goods company, leading an ad hoc team of human resources professionals. We were in the middle of an intense personnel acquisition and integration project, and tight deadlines were piling on pressure from all sides.

One afternoon, during what felt like the hundredth meeting of the week, I noticed that something was off. My usually engaged and enthusiastic team members appeared disengaged and frustrated. Conversations were stilted, body language was closed off, and input on brainstorming was minimal at best. When I reflected later that evening, I recognized it wasn't just them; it was me. The realization was a light bulb moment. My stress and anxiety had started to seep into our interactions.

I had been so focused on meeting deadlines and pushing for results that I neglected to consider my team's well-being and emotional state. Dealing with my own stress in an unhealthy manner inadvertently created a tense work environment. This realization hit hard.

The next morning, I called for a team meeting—not about work tasks or deadlines—but simply to check in with everyone emotionally. I started by sharing my own feelings of stress and pressure. To my surprise, the floodgates opened. My team began to express their sentiments, frustrations, and suggestions freely. This candid conversation nurtured an atmosphere of mutual respect and understanding.

From that day forward, I made a conscious effort to check in with myself regularly and ensure this practice extended to checking in with my team as well. It taught me that self-awareness doesn't just benefit you personally; it dramatically impacts those around you, too.

A Personal Health Wake-Up Call

Another poignant moment of self-awareness came several years ago during a routine doctor's visit. I'd always thought of myself as relatively healthy—no major issues or frequent illnesses—but reality struck hard when my doctor informed me that my lifestyle choices were beginning to catch up with me. My cholesterol levels and blood pressure were high, and I couldn't afford to ignore them any longer.

Later that evening at home, I took a long look in the mirror—both literally and figuratively. Being honest with myself wasn't easy, but it had to be done. Taking stock of what had brought me here, I realized:

- My eating habits had become unbalanced due to long work hours and international travel,
- Exercise was sporadic at best, often sidelined by fatigue or sheer laziness,
- Stress levels were through the roof without any appropriate outlets for relief.

I knew things had to change, but realizing it wasn't enough—I needed action plans grounded in this new self-awareness if I wanted better health outcomes moving forward.

Mapping out incremental changes worked wonders in making these shifts sustainable. For instance:

AREA	OLD HABIT	NEW HABIT
Meal Planning	Fast food & takeouts	Healthier meals
Physical Activity	Skipping workouts frequently	Daily 30-minute walks or workouts
Stress Management	Bottling up emotions	Meditation & open conversations

Incorporating these habits required commitment, but they gradually became second nature as they aligned more closely with an awareness-driven approach toward achieving a better quality of life, rather than merely surviving.

This period taught me invaluable lessons about how critical it is not only knowing "**what**" needs improvement—be it personal health or professional relationships—but truly understanding "**why**" those improvements are crucial adds to the motivation behind gradual yet lasting positive changes moving forward!

Both of these instances underscore the vital importance of self-awareness in achieving true personal growth that transcends mere surface-level changes, adding immense value and profoundly transforming everyday experiences.

WORKSHEET
Assessing Your Level of Self-Awareness

Take a few moments to reflect on the questions below. Write down your thoughts, feelings, and insights honestly. This worksheet is for you to gain clarity and enhance your self-awareness.

Reflection Questions

1. What are my core values? List the principles that guide your life.

Example: Honesty, Compassion, Growth.

_____

_____

_____

_____

_____

2. How do I usually react in stressful situations? Identify patterns in your responses.

Example: Do I get angry, anxious, calm?

_____

_____

_____

_____

3. What triggers strong emotional reactions in me? Recognize what events or interactions often cause intense feelings.

Example: Criticism at work, conflicts with loved ones.

_____

_____

_____

_____

4. How do I handle feedback from others? Reflect on whether you get defensive or take it constructively.

Example: Feeling hurt initially but later understanding the feedback.

_____

_____

_____

_____

5. What are my strengths and weaknesses? List areas where you excel and where you struggle.

Example: Strengths—Empathy, communication; Weaknesses—Procrastination, overthinking.

_____
_____
_____
_____
_____
_____
_____

Strengths:

_____
_____
_____
_____
_____
_____
_____
_____

Weaknesses:

_____
_____
_____
_____
_____

6. What goals make me feel passionate and excited? Write down personal and professional aspirations that inspire you.

Example: Learning a new language, advancing in my career.

_____
_____
_____
_____
_____

7. How do I cope with failure or setbacks? Analyze your coping mechanisms.

Example: Reflecting on lessons learned or feeling discouraged.

_____
_____
_____
_____
_____

Self-Awareness Rating Scale

Rate yourself from 1 to 5 (1 being "Not at all" and 5 being "Very much") based on the following statements:

Statement	Rating (1-5)
I understand my emotions and can pinpoint why I feel a certain way	
I react calmly to stressful situations	
I am aware of my emotional triggers and handle them constructively	
I accept feedback graciously and use it for self-improvement	
I have a clear understanding of my strengths	
I acknowledge my weaknesses and actively work on them	
My personal and professional goals align with my core values	

RATING SCALE: If you rated yourself less than 3 on any item, consider taking action to grow in that area.

ACTION PLAN: Based on your reflections and ratings, identify one or two areas where you'd like to improve your self-awareness. Create an action plan to address these areas:

a. Area for Improvement: Define specifically what you want to work on.

Example: Managing anger in stressful situations.

_____

_____

_____

_____

_____

b. Steps to Take: Bullet out actionable steps you can follow.

Example: Practice deep breathing when feeling stressed. Reflect on the root cause of anger through journaling. Seek feedback from a trusted friend or mentor.

_____

_____

_____

_____

_____

c. Remember, self-awareness is an ongoing journey. Be kind to yourself but be honest as you navigate through it, celebrating small achievements along the way.

_____

_____

_____

_____

_____

2

THE IMPORTANCE OF SELF-REFLECTION

"Self-reflection is the school of wisdom."

~Baltasar Gracián

Self-awareness and self-reflection often go hand in hand, even though they are two distinct concepts. While they rely on each other to some extent, they serve different purposes. As we've seen, self-awareness is the conscious understanding of your thoughts, emotions, and reactions. Self-reflection, on the other hand, is about using that awareness to intentionally pause and think about where you've been, where you are now, and where you want to go. It's about being honest with yourself about your strengths and weaknesses, successes and failures, without beating yourself up over mistakes but learning from them.

Think of it this way: if you drove a car without ever checking the dashboard, you wouldn't know if you were running low on fuel or if there was an issue with the engine. Self-reflection serves as your personal dashboard, helping you check in on your mental and emotional well-being, assess your progress toward goals, and make necessary adjustments along the way.

The Benefits

One of the key benefits of self-reflection is that it helps **increase self-awareness**. By regularly taking the time to think about your actions, feelings, and thoughts, you become more attuned to what makes you tick. This heightened sense of awareness enables you to understand your motivations more clearly and recognize patterns in your behavior that may be holding you back.

For instance, let's say you've been feeling particularly stressed out lately. Through self-reflection, you might realize that this stress isn't just from work pressure but also from neglecting hobbies that bring you joy or not spending enough time with loved ones. Recognizing these patterns can help you make meaningful changes to improve your overall well-being.

Self-reflection is also important in **personal growth**. When you can look at past experiences objectively, it opens the door to learning opportunities. For instance, if a project at work didn't go as planned, reflecting on what happened can help you pinpoint what went wrong. From here, you will be able to develop strategies to handle similar situations better in the future from an informed perspective.

Where To Start

To get started with self-reflection, try setting aside a few minutes each day or week specifically for this purpose. You might find it helpful to keep a journal where you jot down thoughts about recent events or how you're feeling. Ask yourself questions like *"What did I do well today?"* or *"What could I have done differently?"*

Here are some simple reflection prompts you can use:

REFLECTION PROMPT	PURPOSE
What am I grateful for today?	Cultivates gratitude and positivity
What challenges did I face?	Identifies areas for growth
How did I handle those challenges?	Assesses problem-solving skills
What can I learn from today's experiences?	Encourages continuous learning
What am I most proud of?	Highlights achievements

Sometimes, self-reflection can be tough because it requires brutal honesty. It's easy to gloss over our flaws or avoid thinking about uncomfortable experiences. But remember, this isn't about judging yourself; it's about understanding yourself better so that you can become the best version of who you're meant to be.

In addition to fostering personal growth, self-reflection can also enhance your relationships with others. When you're more aware of your own behaviors and emotions, you're better equipped to empathize with others and understand their perspectives. This leads to more meaningful connections and stronger relationships.

So, there it is—self-reflection is like having a heart-to-heart chat with yourself! Next time life gets hectic (and let's face it—when isn't it?), take some time out for self-reflection. Think of it as your chance to hit the *"pause"* button and really tune in to what's going on inside. So, go ahead and grab a pen or, open your notes app, and start reflecting.

Quick Self-Reflection Worksheet

To help you get started with self-reflection, here's a simple worksheet you can use:

1. What am I grateful for today?

_____
_____
_____
_____
_____
_____

2. What challenges did I face today?

_____
_____
_____
_____
_____
_____
_____

3. How did I handle those challenges?

___

4. What can I learn from today's experiences?

___

5. What am I most proud of today?

___

6. How do I feel right now?

_____

_____

_____

_____

_____

7. Have I made progress toward my goals?

_____

_____

_____

_____

_____

8. Is there anything I'd like to do differently tomorrow?

_____

_____

_____

_____

_____

As you complete this worksheet, please be honest with yourself, as this is the only way for self-reflection to be effective. It's not about perfection—it's about gaining insights that can help you grow and thrive.

SELF-REFLECTION TECHNIQUES

As we've established, self-reflection allows you to understand yourself better, guiding you toward a more fulfilling path. Let's explore some techniques that will help you on this journey.

1. Think: What Do You Want to Know?

The first step in any self-reflection process is to ask yourself what you want to understand about yourself. Maybe it's why you feel a certain way, why you react in a certain manner, or what drives your motivations. Taking a moment to ponder these questions sets the stage for deeper insight.

I encourage you to write down these questions somewhere visible, perhaps on a sticky note or in your journal, and revisit them regularly. Whether it's about your goals, values, or why you're feeling a certain way, framing these questions can provide clarity and focus.

2. Practice Gratitude

Gratitude can transform your perspective. It shifts our focus from what we lack to what we already have, opening doors to positive thinking and self-awareness. Each morning or evening, take five minutes to jot down three things you're grateful for. They could be as simple as the warm sunshine or a kind word from a friend. Over time, this practice helps us understand what truly matters and brings joy to our lives.

DAY	GRATEFUL FOR
MON	Morning coffee
TUE	Friendly colleague
WED	Evening walk
THU	Family dinner
FRI	Completed project
SAT	Morning coffee
SUN	Friendly colleague

3. Meditate

Meditation offers a tranquil setting where you can explore your thoughts and feelings with clarity. Find a quiet spot where you won't be disturbed, sit comfortably, close your eyes, and focus on your breathing. Inhale slowly, exhale gently, and let go of any tension with each breath.

You don't need to meditate for hours; even ten minutes can make a difference. Over time, regular meditation fosters mindfulness and deeper self-reflection.

4. Have a Conversation with Yourself

Talking to yourself might sound odd but doing it mindfully can be an excellent reflective practice. Stand in front of a mirror and have an honest conversation about how you're feeling or what's been on your mind lately. You can ask questions like *"Why did I react like that?"* or *"What do I really want?"* Speaking aloud gives voice to inner thoughts and can often lead to surprising insights.

5. Set Your Goals

Goals give direction and purpose to our lives, making them an essential aspect of self-reflection. Start by defining what you want to achieve in various areas of your life—career, relationships, personal growth.

Make these goals specific and actionable. For instance, instead of setting a vague goal like *"be healthier,"* specify it by deciding, *"I will walk 30 minutes every day."* Regularly review your progress towards these goals and adjust them as needed.

GOAL	STEPS	TIMELINE
Learn a new skill	Research courses online	One week
Read more books	Schedule daily reading time	Daily
Exercise regularly	Join fitness class	This month

6. Get Out into Nature

Nature has an incredible way of grounding us and making us feel connected with the world around us. Go for nature walks whenever you can. Breathe in the fresh air, listen to the birds, and just be present.

This connection with nature can clear your mind and offer perspectives you might not have considered otherwise. If you can't get out into a forest or park, even spending time in your garden or sitting by a window with a view of some trees can be beneficial.

7. Seek Feedback from Others

Sometimes, other people can see aspects of ourselves that we might miss. Ask for feedback from trusted friends, family members, or colleagues. Be open to what they have to say—both positive and constructive criticism can provide valuable insights into your behavior and actions.

ASPECT	FEEDBACK	PERSON
Communication	"You could be clearer during team meetings."	Colleague
Time Management	"You handle deadlines well but often take on too many tasks."	Manager
Empathy	"You always listen patiently, and it feels good to talk to you."	Friend

8. Reflect on Past Experiences

Spend some time looking back at your life up to this point. Reflect on both the good times and the challenges you've faced, and as you tackle the challenges, ask yourself questions like:

- ➢ What did I learn from that experience?
- ➢ How has it shaped who I am today?
- ➢ What would I do differently now?

Document these reflections in your journal so you can learn from your history and grow.

9. Create a Vision Board

A vision board is a fantastic visual tool that helps keep your goals and dreams in focus. Gather images, quotes, and symbols that represent where you see yourself in the future—personal aspirations, career milestones, or even emotional states you want to cultivate. Place this board somewhere visible as a daily reminder of what you're working towards.

GOAL CATEGORY	IMAGES/QUOTES INCLUDED
Career	"Top Employee Award," pictures of successful entrepreneurs
Personal Growth	"Embrace Change," images representing meditation and self-care
Relationships	Photos with family/friends, quotes on love and connection

Incorporating self-reflection techniques into your daily routine doesn't have to be overwhelming or time-consuming. Start small with one or two practices that resonate with you, then gradually build upon them. Remember, self-reflection isn't a one-time thing—it's about making continuous progress rather than achieving perfection.

JOURNALING FOR SELF-DISCOVERY

Journaling isn't just about writing down your thoughts and experiences; it's about uncovering who you truly are, understanding your emotions, and discovering your deepest desires, fears, and dreams. It's like having an intimate conversation with yourself—it's private, personal, and insightful. Think about it—when you journal, you create a space where you can unpack whatever is on your mind without any judgment.

Dedicate time each day or week to write down your thoughts, feelings, experiences, and reflections. Writing helps in organizing your thoughts and brings up subconscious insights that might otherwise go unnoticed.

For instance, if you had a hard day at work, you can have an entry like this:

Date: June 15th

Today I felt overwhelmed at work but realized it was because I had not taken any breaks. I need to balance my workload better.

Journaling helps in several ways:

1. **Clarity:** Writing things down allows you to see patterns in your thoughts and behaviors over time. It'll help clarify what really matters to you.

2. **Stress Relief:** Once your worries are written down, they often feel more manageable. It's an effective way to release stress.

3. **Problem Solving:** When faced with dilemmas, journaling lets you brainstorm without pressure.

4. **Growth:** Reviewing past entries shows how much you've grown and learned.

There are many ways to journal, and no one way is the 'right' way. Here are some types I find particularly useful:

1. **Gratitude Journal:** Every day, write about three things you're grateful for. This shifts your focus from what's wrong to what's going right.
2. **Dream Journal:** Keep this by your bed and jot down dreams as soon as you wake up. Dreams can reveal our subconscious thoughts.
3. **Stream-of-Consciousness Journal:** Write continuously for a set period (10-15 minutes), letting whatever comes to mind flow onto the paper without censorship.
4. **Bullet Journal:** Combine planning with journaling in a structured format using bullet points.

You don't need much—a notebook or even digital notes on your phone work fine—just start! Here are some tips to help:

1. **Set Aside Time:** Try making it part of your routine, like after breakfast or before bed.
2. **Create a Comfortable Space:** Choose somewhere peaceful where you won't be disturbed.
3. **Be Honest:** Write like no one else will read it; this makes it easier to be truthful.

Prompts To Kickstart Your Writing

Sometimes, staring at a blank page can be intimidating. Here are some prompts that can help get you started:

1. What am I feeling right now?
2. What did I learn today?
3. If I could talk to my younger self, what would I say?
4. What are my biggest goals and why?
5. If money wasn't an issue, what would I do?

Tracking Progress

Another great benefit of journaling is that it allows you to track your progress over time. For example:

DATE	MOOD	KEY EVENT	INSIGHT OR LESSON
01-01	Happy	Went hiking	Nature clears my mind
01-02	Stressed	Work deadline	Need better planning
01-03	Relieved	Finished project	Accomplishment feels good

HOW JOURNALING CHANGED MY LIFE

I can still remember the day I decided to start journaling. It was a cold winter evening, and I was feeling particularly anxious. I had a lot on my mind and no clear way to sort through the chaos. On a whim, I dug out an old notebook and started writing. At first, it felt odd. I wasn't used to being so candid with myself. But as the days went by, something magical happened: my mind began to clear.

The jumbled thoughts that had been nagging me for weeks seemed more manageable once they were on paper.

Keeping a gratitude journal turned out to be one of the most powerful practices I have ever tried. During a particularly tough week at work, I decided to try writing three things I was grateful for each day. To my surprise, this simple act shifted my entire perspective. Instead of focusing on stressors and anxieties, my mind began zeroing in on small moments of joy—like a kind gesture from a colleague or a cup of hot chocolate on a cold day.

Another notable shift occurred when I began keeping a dream journal. It was fascinating to see patterns emerge from my subconscious thoughts. Those fragmented dreams turned into insightful reflections about fears and desires I didn't even know I had.

After a while, I decided to take it a step further and tried out stream-of-consciousness journaling. There's something incredibly freeing about allowing your mind to wander without trying to control or direct it. At one point, during a 15-minute session, I ended up scribbling about an unresolved conflict with a friend. By the end of those 15 minutes, I had gained clarity on how to approach and resolve the situation amicably.

To track progress over time, I often use a simple chart like this:

DATE	MOOD	KEY EVENT	INSIGHT OR LESSON
01-10	Sad	Argument with friend	Need better communication
01-15	Happy	Weekend getaway	Nature rejuvenates me
01-20	Anxious	Project deadline approaching	Plan ahead for peace of mind
02-01	Content	Finished reading a book	Learning brings happiness

Incorporating these types of entries helped me understand myself better and recognize patterns that needed changing. Journaling has acted like a mirror—reflecting back not just who I am in moments of joy or stress but also who I aspire to be. It's been transformative in ways that are deeply personal yet universally relatable.

I encourage you to take that first step today. Grab any notebook lying around or open your phone's notes app and just start writing. You don't need to have it all figured out; trust in the process and let your words guide you toward greater self-discovery.

Remember, there's no right or wrong way to journal—just your way. Trust yourself enough to be brutally honest in those pages because that honesty can be incredibly liberating.

3

IDENTIFYING YOUR STRENGTHS AND WEAKNESSES

"Accept yourself, your strengths, your weaknesses, your truths, and know what tools you have to fulfill your purpose."

~Steve Maraboli

Let's be honest—sometimes it's easier to spot what we *can't* do than to recognize what we're really good at. But understanding both your strengths and weaknesses is one of the most empowering steps you can take in your personal growth journey. Knowing what you're good at can help you pursue your passions, excel in your career, and build a life that aligns with your strengths. At the same time, recognizing your weaknesses allows you to address them head-on or find ways to work around them. This ensures they don't become hidden obstacles that unknowingly hold you back.

When you know your strengths, you can focus on enhancing them and leveraging them to open new doors. It makes you more confident because you operate within areas where you naturally excel. As you know, confidence is key in both personal and professional settings; it influences how others perceive you and your effectiveness in various roles.

Similarly, being aware of your weaknesses enables you to create effective strategies for improvement. This self-awareness fosters growth, encouraging you to learn new skills or seek help from others when needed. It's a realistic approach that strikes a balance between optimism and pragmatism, making it easier to navigate life's challenges.

SWOT (STRENGTHS, WEAKNESSES, OPPORTUNITIES, THREATS) ANALYSIS

When it comes to truly understanding where we stand in life and where we want to go, a tool called **SWOT Analysis** can be incredibly helpful. SWOT stands for Strengths, Weaknesses, Opportunities, and Threats. Imagine you are on a long road trip. You need to know what your car can do (Strengths), what its limitations are (Weaknesses), the scenic routes and attractions on the way (Opportunities), and the roadblocks or detours you need to avoid (Threats). A SWOT Analysis is much like preparing for that journey. It helps you map out your personal and professional path more effectively.

1. **Strengths**: Think about what you're exceptionally good at—maybe you're an excellent communicator, or perhaps you have a knack for problem-solving. Your strengths are the qualities and abilities that give you an edge over others. These are your built-in advantages that can help you succeed in various aspects of life, from your career to personal relationships.

2. **Weaknesses**: Honestly, none of us like admitting these, but it's crucial if we want to grow. A weakness could be something like procrastination or difficulty in saying no to

people. Recognizing these is just as important as knowing your strengths, because they indicate which areas need improvement.

3. **Opportunities**: Opportunities act like those must-see landmarks on your map. These could be anything from an upcoming work promotion to a new class that can elevate your skills. Recognizing opportunities requires keen observation skills and sometimes a bit of imagination, too.

4. **Threats**: These could be external factors, such as economic downturns that affect your job, or internal ones, like self-doubt that hinders your progress. Identifying threats enables us to develop effective strategies for dealing with them.

A typical SWOT table can look like this:

THE SWOT TABLE			
POSITIVE FACTORS		**NEGATIVE FACTORS**	
STRENGTHS	OPPORTUNITIES	WEAKNESSES	THREATS
Excellent communication	Upcoming promotion	Procrastination	Economic downturn
Problem-solving skills	New skill development classes	Difficulty in saying no	Self-doubt

Taking a look at this table can make everything clearer. On one side you have all the positive factors—your strengths and opportunities; on the other side, you have the undesirable factors—your weaknesses and threats.

WORKSHEET
Analyzing Your SWOT

Creating a SWOT analysis is straightforward but does take some honest self-reflection:

1. List Your Strengths:

What do you excel at?

_____

_____

_____

_____

_____

What do others say about your positives?

_____

_____

_____

_____

_____

What resources do you have?

_____

_____

_____

_____

_____

2. Identify Your Weaknesses:

Where do you need improvement?

_____
_____
_____
_____
_____

What tasks do you avoid because you're not confident doing them?

_____
_____
_____
_____
_____

What habits or negative traits might hold you back?

_____
_____
_____
_____
_____

3. Search for Opportunities:

Are there trends that could benefit you?

_____
_____
_____
_____
_____

Can networking with certain people help?

_____
_____
_____
_____
_____

Are there new skills or knowledge that could advance your journey?

_____
_____
_____
_____
_____

4. Acknowledge Threats:

What obstacles do you face?

_____
_____
_____
_____
_____
_____

Who competes with you for resources or attention?

_____
_____
_____
_____
_____
_____

Is the current climate (economic, social) a threat to your goals?

_____
_____
_____
_____
_____
_____

Once you've identified these key areas, you'll be better equipped to create strategies that leverage your strengths and opportunities, while addressing and mitigating weaknesses and threats.

LEVERAGING STRENGTHS AND OPPORTUNITIES

We all have unique strengths and opportunities that can significantly shape our lives. Going by our previous road trip analogy, let's say you have a powerful, reliable car (your strengths) and a map highlighting exciting destinations along your route (your opportunities). To make the most of your journey, it's important to recognize these assets and leverage them to their fullest potential.

Strengths are those qualities or skills that come naturally to you. They are the things you excel at without much effort. Perhaps you're a great listener, a fantastic planner, or have a knack for problem-solving. Whatever your strengths are, recognizing them is the first step to leveraging them.

Take some time to reflect on what you're good at. Consider the activities you enjoy and excel at. Ask friends, family, or colleagues for their perspectives on your strengths. Sometimes, others can see our strengths more clearly than we can.

Once you've identified your strengths, think about how you can use them more effectively in various areas of your life.

If you're a great communicator, for instance: *how might that help you in your relationships or your career?*

If you're skilled at organizing: *how can that ability assist you in planning and achieving your personal goals?*

Opportunities, on the other hand, are the situations or conditions that can help you move forward toward your objectives. They may include external factors such as job openings, educational programs, or support networks that align with your interests and goals.

Identifying opportunities begins with paying attention to what's happening around you. Stay informed about developments in your areas of interest. *Are there new trends emerging in your field? Are there upcoming events or workshops that could enhance your skills?* Networking can also open doors to new opportunities by connecting you with people who share similar interests or goals.

After recognizing both your strengths and opportunities, the magic happens when you combine the two. For example, if one of your strengths is graphic design and there are opportunities for freelance projects online, use this intel to build a portfolio and grow your client base.

Let's break down this process with some actionable steps:

1. Identify Your Strengths

- Make a list of activities where you excel.
- Seek feedback from trusted individuals.
- Reflect on past successes.

2. Spot Opportunities

- Stay updated with trends in your area of interest.
- Attend events and workshops.
- Network consistently.

3. Align Strengths with Opportunities

- Find intersections between what you're good at and available opportunities.

- Set specific goals using this alignment.
- Take action by starting small and gradually expanding.

Here's an example from my own life. I realized early on that I had a talent for teaching and storytelling (my strength). As I kept an eye out for opportunities, I noticed there was a need for developing and conducting training programs within my company. I volunteered to conduct those programs every chance I got (the opportunity). Combining my strength in teaching others with these opportunities allowed me to develop expertise in people development, which eventually led me to launch my own talent management consulting company!

It's also important to remember that leveraging strengths and opportunities is an ongoing process. Life is dynamic; new strengths emerge as we grow, and fresh opportunities present themselves over time. Be adaptable and always be on the lookout for ways to leverage what you're good at against the backdrop of evolving opportunities.

And now it's your turn! I've created a simple worksheet below that will help guide you through identifying your own strengths and spotting potential opportunities.

WORKSHEET
Identify Your Strengths

1. Skill Survey: List three skills that others have commented on positively about you.

_____

_____

2. Pride Points: Think about moments when you felt proud of something you achieved. What strengths were you using?

_____

_____

_____

3. Flow Moments: When do you lose track of time because you're so absorbed in an activity? These are often your strength areas.

_____

_____

_____

WORKSHEET
Spotting Opportunities

1. Keep Your Eyes Open: List three potential opportunities you've noticed recently.

_____

_____

_____

2. Network Expansion: Who are three people you can reach out to for new opportunities?

_____

_____

_____

3. New Skills Acquisition: What are three skills or knowledge areas that could create more opportunities for you?

_____

_____

_____

The magic happens when we combine our strengths with the opportunities we identify. Imagine being really good at writing (a strength) and then spotting an opening for a guest blog post (an opportunity). By merging the two, you not only showcase your skill but also open doors for further growth.

ACTION STEPS:

1. Reflect on your identified strengths and think about how they align with any upcoming opportunities.
2. Make it a habit to jot down potential opportunities every week.
3. Reach out and connect with people who might lead you to exciting new chances.
4. Practice combining one strength with one opportunity each month.

ADDRESSING AND IMPROVING WEAKNESSES

Why focus on your weaknesses when you could just play to your strengths? Well, think of your weaknesses as tiny hurdles that stand between you and your even greater potential. Overcoming them can open doors to opportunities you'd never imagined. Before you can improve anything, you need to know what needs fixing. This might sound simple but can be a bit tricky. Sometimes, our weaknesses are glaringly obvious—such as a fear of public speaking or a tendency to procrastinate. Other times, they're hidden beneath the surface, like poor listening skills or an inability to accept criticism.

One effective way to identify your weaknesses is through self-assessment tools, such as the SWOT Analysis. Once you've identified your weaknesses, dig a little deeper. Ask yourself why these weaknesses exist. Perhaps your poor listening skills stem from being easily distracted or from anxiety in social situations. Identifying the root cause will provide a clearer path toward improvement.

CREATE AN ACTION PLAN

Identifying and understanding your weaknesses isn't enough; you need an action plan. Here's how you can go about it:

1. **Set Clear Goals:** Be specific about what you want to achieve. If your goal is to improve your public speaking skills, say exactly that.

2. **Take Small Steps:** Break down your goals into manageable tasks. For public speaking, you could start by practicing in front of a mirror before moving on to friends or small groups.

3. **Seek Resources:** There are tons of resources available today—from online courses and books to apps and mentors.

Like any other skill, overcoming weaknesses requires practice. Let's take public speaking as an example again:

1. **Join Groups:** Consider joining clubs like Toastmasters, where everyone is there for the same reason—to improve their public speaking skills.
2. **Watch and Learn:** Platforms like TED Talks can offer valuable insights into how skilled speakers engage their audiences. Watch out for their body language, pacing, level of eye contact and key elements they use to keep people engaged, such as storytelling.
3. **Get Feedback:** Ask for constructive criticism from people you trust.

Tracking your progress is crucial for maintaining motivation and seeing how far you've come. Create a simple chart that outlines what steps you've taken and the results:

ACTIONS TAKEN	OUTCOMES
Practiced speeches in front of mirror	Gained ability to maintain eye contact
Joined Toastmasters	Improved confidence in public speaking
Watched TED Talks	Learned new techniques for audience engagement

4

EMOTIONAL INTELLIGENCE

"We are dangerous when we are not conscious of our responsibility for how we behave, think, and feel."

~Marshall B. Rosenberg

Every day, we experience one emotion after another—happiness, sadness, anxiety, excitement—you name it. However, recognizing these emotions as they arise is not always easy. Feelings can be complicated; they can overlap and sometimes contradict each other. Emotional intelligence helps us sort through and handle our emotions better. At its core, emotional intelligence is the ability to recognize, understand, and manage our own emotions.

The first step in improving emotional intelligence is becoming more aware of these feelings as they appear, and this is where you put your self-awareness into use.

Quick Exercise:

Take a moment and think about today. *Did you feel happy when you saw a friend? Did you get frustrated when you hit traffic on your way to work?* Or maybe you felt proud after completing a task you had been putting off. What made you feel happy, angry, or sad today?

Write your response below:

_____
_____
_____
_____
_____
_____

This exercise offers a brief glimpse into what it takes to be in tune with your emotions.

To enhance your emotional awareness, you can keep an *"emotion journal."* For example:

TIME	SITUATION	EMOTION FELT
8:00 AM	Morning exercise	Energized
9:00 AM	Traffic on the way to work	Frustrated
1:00 PM	Lunch with friends	Joyful
3:00 PM	Deadline approaching	Stressed

Writing down your feelings helps to recognize patterns in your emotional responses. It might sound simple, but articulating your feelings makes them more real and, therefore, more manageable.

Another key aspect of recognizing emotions is understanding what triggers them. Noticing the cause of an emotion allows us to react better in future situations. For instance, if you're feeling anxious right before a presentation, take a moment to ask yourself why this feeling has surfaced. *Is it because you're afraid of speaking in public? Do you feel unprepared?* By identifying the trigger, you can take steps to mitigate it—perhaps through practice or preparation.

Listening to our body's physical responses can also offer clues about our emotions. Feelings are often accompanied by physical signs, such as sweaty palms during stress or a quickened heartbeat during excitement. Take a couple of seconds throughout the day to pause and make note of any physical cues you're experiencing.

Emotion Labeling

Let's talk about labeling emotions accurately. Sometimes, we brush off our feelings lightly or mislabel them because we're unsure what exactly we're experiencing. Cultivating an emotional vocabulary can dramatically improve how we deal with our emotions. Here's a simple list to help broaden your emotional vocabulary:

- Happy (Joyful, Content, Satisfied)
- Sad (Disappointed, Miserable, Grief-stricken)
- Angry (Frustrated, Enraged, Annoyed)
- Afraid (Anxious, Nervous, Terrified)

Once you've recognized and named the emotion accurately, it's time to accept it without judgment. Emotions are neither good nor bad—they just are. Feeling angry or sad doesn't make you a bad person; it makes you human.

Discussing these feelings openly with someone you trust can also lead to better emotional understanding. Communication allows us not only to express ourselves but also to gain others' perspectives, which might illuminate triggers or solutions we hadn't considered.

Lastly—and perhaps most importantly—be kind to yourself during this journey of emotional discovery. We're all navigating complex lives filled with ups and downs. Recognizing your emotions is merely the first step towards handling them better and showing up as your best self in every aspect of life.

One effective practice for becoming more in tune with your emotions is to regularly engage in exercises that prompt introspection and emotional clarity. Next up is a worksheet to help you get started on this journey of emotional recognition.

WORKSHEET
Emotional Awareness

1. Daily Emotion Tracking

Complete the table below each day to track your emotional experiences and their triggers. This will help you identify patterns and become more aware of your emotional landscape *(the table below allows for several entries to get you started, but you can duplicate this in your personal journal for daily tracking)*.

TIME	SITUATION	EMOTION FELT	PHYSICAL RESPONSE	THOUGHTS

2. Reflection Questions

a. What patterns do you see in your emotions? Write down any recurring themes or situations that appear frequently in your emotion tracking table.

_____

_____

_____

_____

b. What are common physical responses you notice? Identify any physical signs that accompany specific emotions. This can include sensations like a racing heartbeat, tension in your muscles, or butterflies in your stomach.

_____

_____

_____

_____

c. How do the thoughts connected to your emotions influence how you feel?

_____

_____

_____

_____

d. Reflect on how your mindset and internal dialogues contribute to the emotions you experience.

_____
_____
_____
_____
_____
_____

e. How can recognizing these patterns help you in future situations?

_____
_____
_____
_____
_____

f. Consider how understanding these patterns might enable you to prepare better for and manage similar future emotional experiences.

_____
_____
_____
_____
_____

3. Emotional Vocabulary Practice

In addition to the vocabulary list we covered earlier, expand your ability to label emotions by practicing with this list:

- Excited: Thrilled, Enthusiastic, Energetic
- Calm: Peaceful, Relaxed, Tranquil
- Confused: Perplexed, Baffled, Uncertain
- Inspired: Motivated, Uplifted, Encouraged

Take a few minutes each day to complete the table and answer the questions thoughtfully. By doing this regularly, you'll begin to notice an improvement in how well you understand and manage your own emotions. Don't rush the process—remember, self-awareness is a continuous journey, and every step forward is progress.

MANAGING EMOTIONAL RESPONSES

Emotions are complex reactions that involve both mind and body. They're often set off by specific events and lead to distinct internal and external reactions. For instance, you might feel a surge of joy when you achieve a goal, which might lead to you working with enthusiasm for the rest of your day. On the other hand, you may feel angry when you are reprimanded by your boss, which can make you feel irritated by the mere sight of your colleagues. Recognizing these emotions and their reactions is the first step in managing them.

One of the keys to managing emotions is identifying what triggers them. Take a moment to think about times you've experienced strong emotions. *Was it during an argument with a loved one? Or maybe when you faced criticism at work?* These are those little (or sometimes big) things that set you off.

Think of emotional triggers like buttons—when pressed, they release a flood of emotions. Like that one comment from your friend that just hits you the wrong way or running late for a meeting, and your heart starts racing.

Here's a pro tip: Grab a notepad and jot down situations that make you feel overly emotional. *Do you get angry when someone cuts you off in traffic? Or maybe you feel anxious when speaking in front of a crowd?* Knowing these triggers is the first step to managing your responses.

BREAKING THE CYCLE OF EMOTIONAL REACTIONS

Got your triggers noted down? Awesome! Now, let's break the cycle. How do we do that?

Step One: Change Your Beliefs

Changing how you react emotionally starts with changing what you believe about the situation. If you think, *"Everyone who cuts me off is disrespecting me,"* you're setting yourself up for anger. Changing your belief to something like, *"Maybe they're in a hurry for an emergency,"* can switch your perspective and dial down those intense emotions.

Step Two: Know Why You Want to Manage Your Emotions

Why is this important to you? Do you want more peace in your life? Maybe healthier relationships? Keep that "**why**" at the forefront of your mind—it'll keep you motivated as you retrain your brain.

You can also put it down on paper to have a tangible reminder.

Step Three: Define Two Situations

Pick two specific situations where you'd like to react differently. Maybe it's staying calm during traffic or showing more compassion when someone messes up at work. Write them down and practice new ways to respond when those situations come up again.

You can use the following space to brainstorm ideas:

Situation	Better Possible Responses

TECHNIQUES FOR MANAGING EMOTIONAL RESPONSES

Now that you've identified your triggers and have an understanding of how to change your beliefs, let's look at some practical techniques:

1. Use the "Pause and Reflect" Strategy

Have you ever found yourself reacting impulsively to a situation only to regret it later? The "Pause and Reflect" strategy can help with that. Whenever you feel overwhelmed by an emotion, take a moment to pause. Don't react immediately.

Give yourself a few seconds—literally count to ten if needed. This allows your brain some time to catch up with your emotions, giving you room to think clearly and respond more thoughtfully.

2. Develop Healthy Outlets

Emotions need an outlet—it's like letting steam out of a pressure cooker. Whether it's through writing, talking to a friend, or engaging in physical activity, find a healthy way to channel your emotions.

For instance, I love taking long walks when I'm feeling stressed—it helps me process my thoughts and release pent-up energy.

3. Reframe Your Thoughts

Our thoughts have a powerful influence on our emotions. If you're feeling negative emotions, try reframing your thoughts. Instead of focusing on what's going wrong, identify any silver linings or positives in the situation. This doesn't mean ignoring reality but finding a more balanced perspective. For example, if you're upset because you made a mistake at work, reframe it as a learning opportunity rather than a failure.

4. Deep Breathing

Deep breathing is an excellent way to manage immediate emotional responses. When we're anxious or angry, our breathing becomes shallow and quickens. Slow, deep breaths can help calm your mind and body almost instantly. Try inhaling deeply through your nose for a count of four, holding it for another four counts. Then, exhale slowly through your mouth for four counts.

Here's a simple technique:

- Sit or lie down comfortably.
- Close your eyes and place one hand on your chest and the other on your abdomen.
- Inhale deeply through your nose, allowing your abdomen to rise while keeping your chest relatively still.
- Exhale slowly through your mouth.

Repeat this process several times until you feel more relaxed.

5. Progressive Muscle Relaxation (PMR)

Progressive Muscle Relaxation is another great tool for managing emotional stress and anxiety. This involves tensing and then slowly relaxing different muscle groups in the body. Start from your toes and work your way up to your head or vice versa.

Here's how you can do it:

- Find a quiet place where you won't be disturbed.
- Sit or lie down in a comfortable position.
- Close your eyes and take a few deep breaths to relax.
- *Start with your feet:* Tense the muscles in your feet as tightly as possible for about 5 seconds.

- *Release:* Slowly relax all tightness in your feet and pay attention to how different they feel when relaxed compared to when they are tense.
- *Move upwards:* Gradually work up through each muscle group (e.g., legs, abdomen, chest, arms), tensing each muscle group for about 5 seconds before releasing the tension.

By systematically tensing and relaxing each muscle group in this manner, you'll likely experience reduced physical tensions, which contributes remarkably towards emotional calmness.

6. Cognitive Reappraisal

Cognitive Reappraisal is about changing the way you think about something that's causing you stress or negative emotions. For example, if you're upset about getting critical feedback at work, instead of seeing it as a personal attack or failure, try reappraising it as an opportunity for growth and improvement. This shift in perspective can significantly reduce emotional distress and help you handle situations more effectively.

EMPATHY AND UNDERSTANDING OTHERS

Empathy is the ability to understand and share the feelings of another person. Empathy is often mistaken for sympathy—feeling sorry for someone. However, it's much deeper and requires you to actually put yourself in their shoes and experience their emotions as if they were your own.

In the rush of everyday life, it's easy to become self-centered and focused on our own issues. But showing up for life calls on us to connect with others in meaningful ways—and empathy is the key that unlocks these deeper connections.

Let's break down empathy into two types: cognitive empathy and emotional empathy.

1. **Cognitive Empathy:** This is the ability to understand how someone else feels and to understand what they might be thinking. With cognitive empathy, it's like you're a detective who can put together clues to comprehend someone else's mental state. Personally, this type of empathy has helped me communicate more effectively because I can easily figure out what words or actions might help or hurt a situation.

2. **Emotional Empathy:** This type goes a step further—beyond just understanding someone's feelings—to actually feeling them yourself. It's the difference between knowing that your friend is sad because their pet died (cognitive) and actually feeling sad along with them (emotional). Emotional empathy connects us at a heart level.

When we practice empathy, several remarkable things happen:

1. **Improved Relationships:** Taking the time to understand others has greatly deepened the quality of my relationships. Naturally, people feel seen, heard, and valued when they realize that we genuinely care about how they feel.

2. **Better Communication:** When I know where someone else is coming from, I find myself choosing my words more thoughtfully and listening with greater intention.

3. **Conflict Resolution:** Empathy makes it easier to step back and understand both sides of an issue, which makes finding common ground less of an uphill battle.

Now, empathy requires both active listening and non-verbal communication skills, such as maintaining eye contact, nodding, and exhibiting responsive body language. Let me explain this through an example: Imagine your friend is telling you about a bad day at work. Instead of jumping in with advice or my own stories, I might say something like, *"That sounds really tough. How did it make you feel?"* and lean in towards them to show that I am attentive. By doing this, I open the door for them to share more deeply.

You've probably heard the phrase, *"Walk a mile in someone else's shoes."* In many ways, that's exactly what empathy is. Walking that metaphorical mile isn't always easy, though; sometimes, it means confronting uncomfortable truths about others or even ourselves. Yet by doing so, we grow as individuals—and those around us benefit too.

Another important aspect is that empathy can be cultivated. It's not something you're either born with or without. Here are some practical steps for nurturing this essential quality:

1. **Be Curious:** Ask open-ended questions about people's lives and really listen to their answers—don't just listen to respond, listen to understand.

2. **Practice Mindfulness:** Being present in the moment helps you tune out external and internal distractions, allowing you to fully focus on others.

3. **Read Diverse Stories:** Books and articles can provide insights into lives and perspectives different from your own, which can broaden your capacity to understand.

4. **Volunteering:** Serving those less fortunate puts you in direct contact with people whose lives and struggles may be vastly different from your own. This can open your eyes to new realities, and not only can it help you build empathy but also another essential quality—compassion.

The benefits of practicing empathy extend beyond individual relationships. It can transform communities and workplaces, creating environments where people feel supported and understood. When empathy is part of the culture, everyone benefits.

To help you cultivate empathy in your daily life, I've created a simple worksheet for practicing active listening and reflection. Use this tool whenever you want to improve your empathetic skills.

WORKSHEET
Building Empathy Skills

1. Recall a recent conversation with a friend or colleague. Write down what they were feeling and why.

_____

_____

_____

_____

_____

2. Describe a situation where you practiced cognitive empathy. What did you understand about the person's thoughts or feelings?

_____
_____
_____
_____
_____

3. Think of a moment when you experienced emotional empathy. How did it make you feel?

_____
_____
_____
_____
_____

4. List three questions you could ask to deepen your understanding of someone else's experience.

_____
_____
_____
_____
_____

5. Identify a character from a book or article you recently read who had a very different life experience than yours. What did that character teach you about empathy?

_____

_____

_____

_____

By making empathy a daily practice, you can enrich your relationships, improve communication, and navigate conflicts with more grace and understanding. Let's make the conscious effort to walk in someone else's shoes and show up for life in the most compassionate way possible.

Need an action plan? The following table is an easy place to start:

EMPATHY ACTION PLAN TABLE		
STEP	ACTION	FREQUENCY
Be Curious	Ask open-ended questions	Daily
Practice Mindfulness	Focus on the present moment	Daily
Read Diverse Stories	Explore books/articles about different lives	Weekly
Volunteer	Serve those less fortunate	Monthly

By implementing these steps, you can cultivate empathy, not only benefiting yourself but also creating a ripple effect that positively impacts everyone around you.

5

MINDFULNESS AND PRESENT-MOMENT AWARENESS

―――•••••―――

"Drink your tea slowly and reverently, as if it is the axis on which the world earth revolves—slowly, evenly, without rushing toward the future; live the actual moment. Only this moment is life."

~Thich Nhat Hạnh

Have you ever done something—like driving, doing the dishes, or walking somewhere—only to realize you have no memory of how you actually did it? If someone asked what you saw during the walk or drive, you'd have no idea. And if you tried to recall how you managed to scrub that greasy pan clean, you'd come up blank, too. We are often guilty of running on autopilot with our minds somewhere else, thinking about what's next or what could have been. But this isn't really "showing up" for life, and we can end up missing out on the sheer joy of life. This is where mindfulness and present-moment awareness come in.

Present-moment awareness is a practice of focusing our attention on what is happening right now. It involves becoming conscious of our actions, feelings, and experiences as they unfold. If you are eating, this means savoring every bite, truly enjoying the flavors and the company you're with, instead of thinking about the next thing on your to-do list. This idea of being fully present in whatever we're doing was beautifully captured by Zen teacher Suzuki Roshi, who said, *"When you eat, you should eat. When you sleep, you should sleep."* It means engaging fully in each activity, whether it's eating, walking, listening to a friend, or even washing dishes.

Mindfulness is directly connected to present-moment awareness. When we talk about mindfulness, we're essentially talking about paying attention to our current experiences without judgment. The developers of the Philadelphia Mindfulness Scale described it as *"the tendency to be highly aware of one's internal and external experiences in the context of an accepting, nonjudgmental stance toward those experiences."* This means recognizing what we feel and see around us without immediately labeling these experiences as good or bad.

A great example is when you are taking a walk in a park. If you're mindful during your walk, you might notice the sound of leaves rustling in the wind, the colors of the flowers blooming around you, and even your breath as it flows in and out. You're not distracted by thoughts about past events or future tasks; you're fully immersed in what you're doing at that moment.

Present-moment awareness is also essential during conversations with friends or family. How often do we catch ourselves thinking about what we want to say next rather than truly listening to the other person? Has this ever affected the quality of your interactions? Probably yes. But as we practice present-moment awareness, we can become better listeners and more empathetic friends.

Another scenario could be at work. Instead of multitasking—for instance, answering emails while participating in a meeting—we can focus solely on one task at a time. This not only makes us more efficient but also reduces stress since our minds aren't pulled in multiple directions.

Here's a simple chart to show how these concepts interlink:

SITUATION	PRESENT-MOMENT AWARENESS BENEFITS
Eating	Savoring flavors; enjoying company
Walking in a park	Noticing nature; feeling relaxed
Conversations	Better listening; more empathy
Work	Increased efficiency; reduced stress

By paying attention to these everyday moments with full awareness and without judgment, we begin to appreciate life's simple joys more deeply and foster better connections with ourselves and others.

TECHNIQUES FOR STAYING PRESENT

Let's say you're hanging out with friends or family or even just enjoying a quiet cup of coffee by yourself. Now, consider how much more meaningful and enjoyable these moments can be if you're fully present, soaking it all in. When we focus on what's happening at the moment, we create richer experiences and deeper connections.

Being present also helps reduce stress. When we constantly think about the past or worry about the future, stress can accumulate, which can be detrimental to our well-being. Staying in the moment allows our minds a break from the endless cycle of thoughts. Plus, it enhances our ability to handle whatever comes our way because we're not caught up in what-ifs or regrets.

To master staying present, try out the following techniques:

1. Meditation

We've mentioned meditation a few times already, but it's worth repeating—when it comes to staying grounded in the present moment, few practices are more powerful. Now, meditation isn't all about emptying your mind or achieving enlightenment under a Bodhi tree. It's about training our minds to focus and be still, even if it's just for a few minutes each day. You don't need any fancy equipment either. Just find a quiet spot where you won't be disturbed.

Sit comfortably—no need for those twisty pretzel poses unless you're into that! Close your eyes and focus on your breathing. You might find it helpful to count your breaths: inhale—1, exhale—2, and so on up to 10, then start again at 1. If your mind wanders, which we know it will, gently bring it back to the breath without judgment.

2. Breath Awareness

Whenever you feel overwhelmed or scattered, pause and take three deep breaths. Feel the air filling your lungs and see if you can notice the temperature change as you inhale and exhale. You'd be surprised how much this simple act brings you back to the present moment! Try setting reminders on your phone to check in with your breath throughout the day.

3. Body Scan

This one is great if you're feeling disconnected from yourself—a common issue when we're rushing around all day. Lie down comfortably or sit in a chair if you're at work. Focus on your toes and work your way up. Notice how each part of your body feels: *Are there any areas of tension or discomfort?* Simply observe without trying to change anything.

A neat trick here is pairing this with breath awareness. As you breathe in, imagine sending your breath to tense areas; as you breathe out, visualize releasing that tension. It'll make you feel like you've just gotten a mini-massage!

4. Grounding Techniques

Grounding techniques are kind of like emergency tools in our mindfulness toolkit. These are perfect when you're spiraling into anxiety or just feeling untethered. One popular method is the 5-4-3-2-1 exercise:

- 5: Name five things you can see around you.
- 4: Touch four things and describe their textures.
- 3: Identify three sounds you can hear.
- 2: Notice two different smells.
- 1: Focus on one thing you can taste.

This method engages all five senses, yanking you right back into the here and now.

5. Mindful Walking

This one's incredibly versatile—you can do it while strolling through a park or even walking from one room to another at home. Focus on each step: how your foot feels hitting the ground, how your muscles engage with each movement, even how the air feels against your face as you walk. The key here is attention; lock into every detail of what you're doing.

6. Mindful Listening

Ever notice how an amazing song can instantly lift your moods? Or how someone's voice can soothe your worries? That's the power of mindful listening. This practice involves fully tuning into sounds—whether it's music, the rustling of leaves, or a friend's words.

Next time you're listening, try to focus solely on the sounds without letting your mind wander. Pay attention to each note, rhythm, or inflection in someone's voice. You can even practice this during conversations by truly listening to what the other person is saying rather than planning your response.

7. Mindful Eating

Who doesn't love food? But often, we're so distracted while eating that we miss out on the full experience. Mindful eating is about being grateful for your meal and savoring every bite.

Start by paying attention to the color and smell of your food before you even take a bite. And when you do, notice the textures and flavors as you chew slowly. Not only will this make your meals more enjoyable, but it may also aid digestion!

Eating mindfully has been a transformative experience for me personally! Sitting down properly at meal times, rather than eating on the go, allows me to better appreciate the flavors and textures by chewing each bite slowly and thoroughly, which has also done wonders for my digestion too!

8. Being in Nature

There's something incredibly grounding about being out in nature. Whether it's a walk in the park or sitting by a lake, nature has a calming effect on our minds.

Try to spend some time outdoors daily. Observe the shapes of clouds, listen to birds chirping, or feel the wind on your skin while keeping your mind free from any thoughts. Just five minutes outside can reset your mind and bring you back to the present.

9. Art

Art has a unique way of pulling us into the moment. Whether it's drawing, painting, or even coloring in an adult coloring book, engaging in creative activities can be incredibly grounding.

You don't have to be a professional artist to benefit from this technique. Don't worry about creating a masterpiece; focus on the process instead of the end result. Notice how your hand moves across the paper or how colors blend together. It's quite soothing and meditative.

INTEGRATING MINDFULNESS INTO DAILY ROUTINE

In our busy lives, finding moments to pause and be present can transform everyday routines into meaningful experiences. By incorporating mindfulness into our daily tasks, we can become more resilient and enhance our overall well-being. Let's see how bringing mindfulness into simple activities can make a big difference:

1. Mindfulness While Brushing Your Teeth

Brushing your teeth is usually something you do on autopilot. Next time you pick up that toothbrush, take a moment to really be in the moment.

Feel the bristles against your teeth and gums. Notice the minty taste of the toothpaste. Pay attention to each movement and how it cleans your teeth bit by bit. Even though it only takes a couple of minutes, you'll start your day feeling centered.

2. Mindfulness While Taking a Shower

Showers are a perfect opportunity for mindfulness. The next time you step into the shower, focus on how the water feels on your skin. *Is it warm? Cool? How does the soap lather up as you clean yourself?* Listen to the sound of water hitting different surfaces.

As you pay attention to these sensations, you'll notice your shower time slowly transforming from a routine activity into a rejuvenating experience.

3. Mindfulness While Commuting to Work

Whether you're driving or using public transportation, commuting offers another chance to practice mindfulness. If you're driving, pay close attention to the road, the hum of the engine, and your surroundings.

If you're on a bus or train, notice your breath and how your body feels seated or standing. Look out the window and appreciate the scenery rather than getting lost in thought or staring at your phone.

4. Mindfulness While Washing the Dishes

Washing dishes can be both mundane and meditative at the same time. Instead of rushing through it, focus on each dish individually. Feel the temperature of the water and the texture of the soap suds on your hands. Listen to the clinking sounds as you place dishes on the rack.

It may seem trivial, but this careful attention can transform a chore into something almost peaceful.

5. Mindfulness While Waiting in Line

Waiting in line is one of those things we all have to endure from time to time—at grocery stores, banks, coffee shops, you name it. Instead of getting antsy or reaching for your phone, take this moment as a mini mindfulness session.

Observe the people around you without judgment. Notice any physical sensations in your body, such as tension or relaxation, and make small adjustments as needed—like relaxing your shoulders or unclenching your jaw.

6. Mindfulness While Observing Your Thoughts

Our minds tend to race with thoughts throughout the day—some important, some trivial. Practicing mindfulness involves observing these thoughts without becoming attached to them.

When you catch yourself worrying or daydreaming, take a deep breath and let that thought pass by like a cloud floating in the sky.

7. Mindfulness During Exercise

Exercise is another area where mindfulness can be profoundly beneficial. Whether I'm running, doing yoga, or lifting weights, focusing on each movement helps me stay present and avoid injury.

I pay attention to my breath, notice how my muscles feel as they contract and expand, and immerse myself entirely in the activity. This mindful approach not only enhances the physical benefits of exercise but also makes it a form of moving meditation.

8. Mindfulness While Working

Work can easily become overwhelming, especially with deadlines and tasks piling up. For me, integrating mindfulness into work involves setting intentional breaks to check in with myself. I also ensure that I focus on one task at a time, rather than multitasking, and pay full attention to whatever I'm doing.

Short pauses to breathe deeply and stretch also keep me balanced and productive, reducing stress throughout the day. The secret is finding what works best for you and sticking to it.

WORKSHEET
Practicing Mindfulness

Take a few moments each day to reflect on your mindfulness practice using the table below.

DAILY ACTIVITY	WHAT DID I NOTICE?	HOW DID IT MAKE ME FEEL?
Brushing your teeth		
Taking a shower		
Commuting		
Washing dishes		
Waiting in line		
Observing thoughts		
Eating		
Exercising		
Working		
Engaging with others		

Reflecting regularly will help reinforce these mindful habits and ensure they become a natural part of your daily routine.

PART II
HAVE A SENSE OF HUMOR

6

THE POWER OF LAUGHTER

"Like a welcome summer rain, humor may suddenly cleanse and cool the earth, the air and you."

~Langston Hughes

Have you ever had a really tough day at work, but then someone cracks a joke and suddenly everything seems more *manageable?* That's the magic of humor. Humor isn't just about making people laugh; it's actually a key ingredient for success, both personally and professionally.

On a personal level, humor has the amazing ability to connect people and can do wonders for your relationships. When you share a laugh with someone, it creates an instant bond. Think about your best friendships or your family gatherings. They're probably filled with inside jokes, funny stories, and lots of laughter. That's because humor helps build trust and fosters closeness. When you laugh with someone, you're sharing a positive experience that can make your relationship stronger. Also, when humor is involved, icebreakers or awkward situations become easier to navigate.

SCIENTIFIC STUDIES ON HUMOR AND ITS BENEFITS

One of the most compelling scientific studies on humor was conducted by Dr. Lee Berk and Dr. Stanley Tan at Loma Linda

University in California. They discovered that laughter decreases stress hormones and increases the number of immune cells and infection-fighting antibodies. This means that when we laugh, our bodies becomes more equipped to fight off illnesses.

Keep in mind that laughter isn't just a response to something funny; it's actually a social signal that we are positively engaging with others. According to a study published in the National Library of Medicine, laughter is 30 times more likely to occur in social contexts than when we're alone. This idea reinforces how indispensable human interaction is for our mental health.

But how exactly does humor benefit us?

For one, it can **improve heart health**. A 2005 study presented at the European Society of Cardiology found that individuals who laugh regularly had improved vascular function compared to those who rarely laughed.

Additionally, humor has **cognitive benefits**. Research by Dr. Rod A. Martin from the University of Western Ontario suggests that humor improves various types of thinking and reduces stress levels, which can improve performance on creative problem-solving tasks.

Have you ever noticed how, after a good laugh, you feel lighter? That's because laughter triggers the **release of endorphins**—natural feel-good chemicals—while reducing the levels of the stress hormone cortisol. This isn't just psychological; it's physiological too. The release of endorphins can create a sense of euphoria similar to what's known as *"runner's high,"* making us feel genuinely happy and relaxed. Endorphins can also help ease pain, so laughing is a great natural painkiller. Additionally, laughter can increase the production of antibodies, hence giving our immune system a boost. Basically, laughter is like free medicine.

As we've touched on, humor can also foster stronger relationships. According to research from Robert Provine, shared laughter plays an essential role in forming bonds between people. It's no wonder why comedians often say that laughter is universal—it truly brings people together.

Another crucial area where humor shines is mental health. Studies published in the International Journal of Geriatric Psychiatry illustrate that humor therapy reduces agitation in elderly patients with dementia and improves emotional well-being.

It's worth mentioning that not all types of humor are beneficial for everyone at every time—something called "***negative***" or "***aggressive***" humor can be harmful or even backfire depending on context and timing. However, light-hearted jokes or simply finding amusing moments during challenging times can serve as a potent coping mechanism.

So next time you find yourself stressed out or feeling down, try watching your favorite comedy show or spending some time with friends who make you laugh. You'll likely find that those moments provide much-needed relief from whatever is weighing you down.

WORKSHEET
Reflection on Humor in Your Life

Take a few moments to think about the role of humor in your life. Reflect on the questions below and jot down your thoughts.

1. How often do you laugh in a typical day?

_____
_____
_____
_____

2. Think of a time when humor helped you connect with someone new. What happened?

_____
_____
_____
_____
_____
_____

3. Describe a situation where a joke or funny story helped to ease tension.

_____
_____
_____
_____
_____

4. Do you use humor in your work environment? If yes, how does it help?

_____

_____

_____

_____

_____

5. Can you recall an instance when laughter improved your mood or handled stress better?

_____

_____

_____

_____

_____

6. What types of humor resonate the most with you? (e.g., puns, sarcasm, anecdotes, etc.)

_____

_____

_____

_____

_____

7. Are there specific people in your life who always make you laugh? How do they do it?

_____
_____
_____
_____
_____
_____
_____
_____

8. How do you feel after sharing a hearty laugh with friends or family?

_____
_____
_____
_____
_____
_____
_____
_____

Now, consider making a humor plan to incorporate more laughter into your daily routine:

MY HUMOR PLAN	
DAY	ACTIVITY TO INCORPORATE HUMOR
MON	
TUE	
WED	
THU	
FRI	
SAT	
SUN	

Remember, humor is not just about jokes—it's about finding joy in everyday moments. Filling out this worksheet can help you recognize how important humor is and how to bring more of it into your life.

ACTION PLAN
Strategies To Cultivate A Sense Of Humor

As we've gathered, humor isn't just reserved for comedians—it's an essential life skill that can lift your spirits, enhance relationships, and even bolster your mental and physical health. It isn't about telling jokes all the time but about adopting a playful attitude that makes life more enjoyable for you and those around you. When you have a sense of humor, you can see the lighter side of life and not taking things too seriously—which is vital for your emotional and mental health.

Here are some actionable strategies you can incorporate into your daily life to nurture your sense of humor:

1. Surround Yourself with Humor: One of the easiest ways to become funnier is to immerse yourself in humor.

- *a. Read Funny Books:* Look for comedic novels or collections of funny essays.
- *b. Watch Comedies:* Spend some downtime with sitcoms or stand-up comedy specials.
- *c. Follow Funny People:* On social media, follow comedians or channels that post humorous content.

2. Learn to Laugh at Yourself: Taking oneself too seriously is often the biggest barrier to developing a sense of humor.

- *a. Share Your Embarrassing Moments:* When you share these moments openly, it normalizes them and makes it easier to laugh about them.
- *b. Practice Self-Deprecation in Moderation:* Make light-hearted jokes at your own expense without being overly harsh.

3. Practice Observational Humor: Observational humor involves finding something funny in everyday situations.

- *a. Keep a Journal:* Write down funny incidents or witty remarks you come across each day.

    b. Observe and Reflect: Take time to notice quirks in your environment or habits people (including yourself) have, and find gentle ways to highlight their humorous aspects.

4. Engage with Playful People: Being around playful people can encourage you to lighten up.

    a. Find a Funny Friend Group: Connect with friends who have a good sense of humor.

    b. Join Clubs or Groups Focused on Fun Activities: Comedy clubs or improv groups are perfect examples.

5. Try New Experiences: Exposing yourself to new environments can restore your sense of wonder—and often result in funny stories!

    a Travel if Possible: Being in unfamiliar places invites humorous mishaps.

    b. Take Up Hobbies That Involve Interaction: Activities like dance classes or team sports contain built-in opportunities for laughter as everyone learns together.

6. Use Positive Affirmations: Sometimes it's helpful to mentally prepare yourself to embrace humor more fully.

    a. Daily Reminders: Start your day by committing that today, you'll find light-hearted moments.

    b. Affirmations Examples:

- "I am open to laughter and joy."
- "I find something funny in my daily life."

7. Adopt a 'Yes, and' Attitude: The concept of "Yes, And," from improv comedy, encourages acceptance and building upon ideas rather than shutting them down. This approach can help you view situations more positively and find humor even in unexpected scenarios.

> *a. Practice Agreement and Addition:* When someone says something, practice agreeing with them and then adding your twist. For instance, if someone talks about their dog's mischief, agree and share a funny story about a pet or situation you've experienced.
>
> *b. Role-play Scenarios:* Engage in playful role-plays with friends or family where you both build upon each other's narrative without saying "no."

8. Look for the Silver Lining: Often, difficult situations can later be viewed from a humorous perspective.

> *a. Reframe Problems:* Instead of seeing challenges as setbacks, look at them as opportunities for funny stories.
>
> *b. Find Humor Amidst Challenges:* Even in stressful moments like getting lost or missing an appointment, look for the lighter or absurd elements that could be funny later.

9. Share Laughter: Sharing laughter with others not only strengthens relationships but also helps you appreciate humor more openly.

a. *Create Opportunities to Laugh Together:* Participate in activities where you're likely to laugh together, like game nights or watching comedy movies.

b. *Casual Joke Sharing:* Make it a habit to share jokes or funny incidents with your friends and family, fostering a culture of laughter around you.

10. Be Playful with Language: Puns, wordplay, and light-hearted teasing can refine your sense of humor.

a. *Word Games:* Engage in games like Scrabble or Pictionary, where humorous language naturally emerges.

b. *Play with Words:* Experiment with puns or clever quips during conversations to make interactions more enjoyable.

Cultivating a sense of humor is about integrating playful and positive practices into your life. Remember, the goal isn't coming up with the perfect jokes or "mastering" humor—it's all about progress towards enjoying life more fully, one laugh at a time.

7

HUMOR IN SOCIAL INTERACTIONS

"A person without a sense of humor is like a wagon without springs. It's jolted by every pebble on the road."

~Henry Ward Beecher

Whether it's a family dinner or a first date, humor is a powerful social tool that helps us bond with others and create memories that truly stick around. Think about it—some of your best memories likely involve hearty laughs with your friends, family, or even a stranger.

Humor also makes tense situations more manageable and reduces anxiety. For example, cracking a joke in a new group can help ease tensions, break down walls and make everyone feel more comfortable. On a personal level, when you laugh at your mistakes or find humor in challenging situations, it becomes easier to cope with life's ups and downs.

Humor can also be a means to enhance communication. A well-placed joke or witty comment can make conversations more engaging and enjoyable. It grabs attention and keeps people interested in what you have to say.

Alonzo Johnson, Ph.D.

USING HUMOR TO BUILD CONNECTIONS

When I think about some of the best connections I've made in life, one common thread is humor. Maybe it was a joke shared in an awkward situation or a funny story that broke the ice at a party. No matter the setting, laughter has an undeniable way of bringing people together.

Back in college, I realized how humor could turn strangers into friends. I remember walking into my freshman dorm and feeling like a fish out of water. Everything was new, and everyone seemed to know what they were doing—except me. On my first day, as we were all getting to know each other, someone told a joke about the terrible cafeteria food. It wasn't even that great of a joke, but it did its job—it made us laugh. Suddenly, the room felt lighter, and conversations started flowing with ease.

Using humor to build connections isn't about being a stand-up comedian or cracking jokes every few minutes. It's all about being genuine and finding moments of lightness in the middle of everyday life. One effective way I've used humor is through self-deprecation—making fun of myself in non-serious ways. It sends the message that I'm not taking myself too seriously, which tends to make others feel more comfortable and at ease around me.

For example, if I'm in a new work environment where things are tense, I might say something like, *"Alright team, let's aim to be less confused than me by the end of the day!"* It always loosens people up and paves the way for open communication. I remember another moment early in my career during my first big presentation. I made a small mistake with the slides, and trust me—it was mortifying at that moment! Instead of fumbling through an apology, I turned it into something humorous. I simply said, *"Looks like even technology thinks Mondays should be optional!"* Everyone laughed, and what could've been an incredibly awkward situation transformed into something everyone could relate to and enjoy.

Here's why humor works so well for building connections:

1. **It Creates Common Ground:** Humor has this fantastic ability to create a shared experience. When two people laugh at the same thing, they feel an instant bond.

2. **It Relieves Stress:** Laughter is scientifically proven to reduce stress levels by releasing endorphins—our body's natural feel-good chemicals.

3. **It Builds Trust:** Sharing a good laugh requires vulnerability on both ends—a trait that's crucial for building trust.

4. **Enhances Communication:** When people are laughing together, they're more likely to be open and honest.

Keep in mind that humor isn't just limited to personal or professional circles; it also plays a massive role in larger settings like community gatherings or social events. Remember when all events moved online due to the pandemic? People found creative ways to insert humor into virtual meetings through funny backgrounds or memes shared during chats—it kept everyone engaged and fostered a sense of solidarity even when physically apart.

In case you're still skeptical about incorporating humor into your interactions because you're not naturally 'funny', don't worry! Here are some simple tips:

1. **Observe**: Pay attention to what makes people around you laugh.

2. **Start Small:** Use light-hearted comments rather than going for elaborate jokes.

3. **Be Relatable:** Share real-life stories or everyday mishaps.

4. **Mind Your Timing:** Sometimes it's not about what you say but when you say it—understanding your timing can make all the difference.

5. **Be Yourself:** Authenticity shines through more than anything else; trying too hard tends to fall flat.

APPROPRIATE AND INAPPROPRIATE HUMOR

So what makes humor appropriate? At its core, it's about being inclusive and considerate. Good humor doesn't single out individuals or groups based on aspects such as race, gender, religion, or other personal characteristics. Instead, it often targets universal experiences that most people can relate to and find funny.

One solid example of appropriate humor is self-deprecating jokes. These are jokes where you poke fun at yourself. It shows that you're humble and don't take yourself too seriously. For instance, I once attempted to cook a gourmet meal but ended up with something that looked more like dog food than haute cuisine. Laughing at our own foibles can humanize us and make us more relatable, as I discovered while presenting the food to my dinner guest as a meal fit for the dog pound. Everyone found humor in the joke and thought the food was tasty nonetheless.

On the other hand, inappropriate humor often disregards the feelings or experiences of others, targeting sensitive subjects or making fun of someone else's misfortune. Jokes that lean towards racism, sexism, ageism, or any form of discrimination usually fall under this category. Instead of bringing people together, these jokes tend to create discomfort and alienation.

APPROPRIATE HUMOR	INAPPROPRIATE HUMOR
Self-deprecating jokes	Racist/sexist jokes
Light-hearted teasing with consent	Making fun of someone's appearance
Situational observations	Jokes about traumatic events
Puns and wordplay	Jokes targeting specific religious beliefs

Aspects of Appropriate Humor

Now let's touch on several crucial aspects of appropriate humor, starting with **_timing_** and **_context_**. Even benign jokes can land poorly if delivered at the wrong time or in an unsuitable context. For example, cracking a joke during a serious business meeting or at a funeral is likely to be seen as inappropriate because it doesn't respect the gravity of the situation.

Similarly, **_knowing your audience_** is important. What might be funny among close friends might not be suitable for a workplace setting or among acquaintances who don't know you well enough to understand your intent. I learned this the hard way when I told a joke to a new work team that my family finds hilarious—dead silence followed. Lesson learned: every group has its boundaries and shared histories that shape what they deem funny.

Tone also plays a huge role in determining appropriateness. A joke told with sarcasm or bitterness might come across as an attack rather than an attempt to lighten the mood. Ensuring your tone conveys friendliness and goodwill helps others receive it the way you meant it.

Interestingly enough, **cultural differences** heavily influence what is considered appropriate versus inappropriate humor. Some cultures value directness and may appreciate humor that others see as blunt or insensitive. Learning about cultural norms when interacting with people from different backgrounds can prevent potential misunderstandings.

One thing that I found invaluable when it comes to appropriate humor is **empathy**. Before making a joke at someone's expense or touching on delicate topics, consider how you'd feel if you were on the receiving end of that joke. Empathy helps us gauge whether our humor is likely to build bridges or burn them.

Lastly, subjects like **politics, religion, and death** can be tricky. They are often tied to personal beliefs and strong emotions. Unless you're with people you know well and who share your sense of humor and views on these topics, it's wise to steer clear of making jokes about them in casual settings.

CONTEXT	APPROPRIATE HUMOR	INAPPROPRIATE HUMOR
Family Gatherings	Light-hearted stories about shared experiences	Targeted jokes about someone's personal matters
Workplace	Relatable workplace anecdotes	Jokes about employees' abilities or personal life
Multicultural Events	Neutral topics like weather, hobbies	Culture-specific jokes that could be misinterpreted
Difficult Times	Gentle humor to lighten the mood	Making light of the situation's seriousness

HANDLING AWKWARD SITUATIONS WITH HUMOR

We've all been there—stuck in an awkward moment that makes us want to disappear. The good news is, you don't need to vanish; you can use humor as a tool to defuse the tension and navigate through such situations with ease. Using humor effectively in awkward moments requires some finesse and a touch of strategy, but it's doable for anyone willing to learn.

1. Make Sure Everyone is in on the Joke

The foundational rule of using humor to handle awkward situations is ensuring that everyone involved gets the joke. If you're the only one laughing, it can make things worse, not to mention a little humiliating for you. For example, if you trip and fall in a crowded room, making a light-hearted comment like, *"I guess gravity wanted to be noticed today,"* can bring relief to everyone watching, including yourself. However, if you make a joke at someone else's expense in such a situation, such as saying, *"At least I didn't break an ankle like poor Joe,"* it could escalate rather than defuse the tension.

One way to ensure everyone is on the same page is by using inclusive language and relatable experiences. Instead of saying, *"Well, someone doesn't know how to walk properly,"* which singles you out negatively, you might say, *"Ah, we've all had days like this!"* This shifts the focus from your individual blunder to something universally relatable.

2. Don't Use Humor to Cover Up Other Emotions

One thing to always keep in mind is that humor should not be used to cover up genuine feelings like anger, sadness, or disappointment. Using it that way can lead to misunderstandings and resentments because people may not take your emotions seriously. Instead, address your primary emotion openly and then use humor to lighten the mood afterward.

Let's say that you're upset because a friend forgot your birthday. Rather than making a sarcastic comment like, *"Oh great, I see how much I matter,"* which can come off as passive-aggressive, express your feelings first: *"I was really looking forward to celebrating with you."* Then follow up with humor if appropriate: *"Guess I'll have twice the fun next year!"* By being transparent about your feelings first, humor becomes a tool for letting go rather than hiding what's genuinely bothering you.

3. Develop a Smarter Sense of Humor

A smarter sense of humor relies on wit, timing, and emotional awareness rather than relying on old cliches or potentially offensive jokes. This means moving beyond slapstick or simple jokes and learning how to read the room for emotional cues.

When I find myself in an awkward situation—like forgetting someone's name at an event—I've learned to gracefully recover with humor that's respectful yet clever: *"I'm terrible with names but wonderful with faces! Remind me again?"* This kind of witty humor shows humility without making others uncomfortable.

Here's a simple chart outlining Dos and Don'ts when using smarter humor in awkward situations:

DOS	DON'TS
Use self-deprecation	Use offensive language
Be situationally aware	Make personal attacks
Test the waters with light jokes	Dive right into sarcasm
Share amusing anecdotes	Rely on outdated stereotypes

4. Tap into Your Playful Side

Sometimes situations call for nothing more than playful banter or an impromptu game—the kind of thing that reminds everyone involved that life doesn't always have to be taken seriously.

Say you're at a formal dinner and accidentally spill your drink. Instead of sinking into embarrassment, playfully invite others into your moment: *"Anyone care for a splash zone experience?"* or make it an impromptu game: *"Let's see who can help me clean this up fastest—go!"* Actively engaging your playful side helps turn potentially mortifying moments into situations that everyone can laugh about. I've found that tapping into your playful side not only defuses tension but also strengthens connections with others. It creates a sense of connection that's hard to replicate with just words.

The Office Meeting Mix-Up

One of my most memorable awkward moments occurred during an office meeting. I had recently joined a new team, and we were having our first big brainstorming session. Everyone was sharing their ideas, and I wanted to make a good impression. So, I decided to propose what I thought was a brilliant suggestion. As I confidently presented my idea, I noticed the room became unusually silent, and people exchanged puzzled looks.

It was only then that I realized my mistake—I had mixed up the project details with another one we weren't discussing that day. My face turned expressionless, and I braced myself for the embarrassment to sink in. In that moment, instead of panicking or retreating into silence, I chose to lighten the atmosphere. *"Well,"* I said with a smile, *"I guess if we ever need ideas for our next project, I'm all set!"* The room burst into laughter, and the tension dissipated immediately.

That experience taught me a valuable lesson: **Mistakes are opportunities for humor and connection.** By playfully acknowledging my blunder, I not only saved face but also delighted my colleagues. We all went back to brainstorming with renewed energy.

The Family Gathering Faux Pas

Family gatherings can be ripe with awkward moments, especially when new partners and long-lost relatives enter the mix. During a recent family gathering, my cousin brought along her new boyfriend. As we were introduced, I mistakenly called him by her ex-boyfriend's name—not once but twice!

Cringe-worthy as it was, instead of pretending it didn't happen or letting the awkward air linger, I decided to address it head-on with humor. *"Looks like someone needs an update on their family cheat sheet!"* I joked while giving myself a mock facepalm.

Everyone chuckled, including my cousin's boyfriend, who seemed relieved that the tension had been broken. The light-hearted acknowledgment turned what could have been an uncomfortable situation into an icebreaker.

What did I learn from this? Humor makes mistakes easier for everyone to bear, especially in social settings where relationships matter deeply. By using self-deprecating humor and making light of my error, I reassured everyone (including myself) that it's okay to make mistakes.

Lessons Learned

Using humor to navigate awkward situations isn't just about quick thinking—it's about how you choose to view those moments and engage others in them. Here's a recap of key strategies:

STRATEGY	APPLICATION
Acknowledge the Mistake Playfully	Turn errors into shared experiences
Use Self-Deprecation	Lighten the mood at your own expense
Create Connectivity	Build rapport through shared laughter
Shift Focus	Redirect attention in relatable ways

Remember, the goal isn't trying to be a comedian but to use humor as a tool for connection and relief in awkward situations. Whether you're at work or among family, these simple strategies can help you handle life's inevitable stumbles with grace and laughter.

8

HUMOR IN THE WORKPLACE

"Laugh as much as possible, always laugh. It's the sweetest thing one can do for oneself & one's fellow human beings."

~Maya Angelou

As we've established, laughter is a natural stress reliever. In an environment where deadlines are tight and workloads can get overwhelming, a good laugh can act as a pressure valve, releasing built-up tension. When we laugh, our body releases endorphins, often referred to as ***"feel-good"*** hormones. These create an overall sense of well-being and can even temporarily relieve pain.

Contrary to what most people may think, being funny at work is not unprofessional—it can actually make you more successful and productive and lead to a generally positive work culture!

If you think about it, who wouldn't want to work in an environment where laughter is valued? It makes everyone feel part of a community rather than just cogs in a machine. It's simple—when you're happy at work, your overall quality of life improves dramatically.

I've always believed that a little laughter goes a long way, especially at work. If you're wondering why humor is so vital in a professional setting, let me break it down for you:

1. **Building Stronger Connections:** Humor helps in building stronger connections among colleagues. You know those times when you share a joke with someone and immediately feel closer to them? This happens at work too. When people laugh together, they form bonds that can significantly enhance teamwork and collaboration. It's like the social glue that makes working together so much smoother.

2. **Reducing Stress**: We all know work can be stressful. Deadlines, challenging tasks, and even occasional friction with co-workers can cause anxiety. But here's where humor steps in as the perfect antidote. When we laugh, our brains release endorphins—those feel-good chemicals that reduce stress and make us feel relaxed. I've found that a good laugh during a rough day can be incredibly rejuvenating.

3. **Boosting Creativity**: You'd be surprised how a humorous environment can spark creativity. When people are relaxed and enjoying their time, they're more likely to think outside the box and come up with innovative ideas. Studies have shown that humor encourages divergent thinking, which is a key part of the creative process. In my experience, brainstorming sessions where everyone is relaxed and laughing tend to produce the best ideas.

4. **Improving Communication**: Humor also plays a substantial role in improving communication in the workplace. It can break down barriers and make it easier for people to express their thoughts freely without fear of judgment. I always find that using humor helps in delivering feedback or addressing sensitive issues without causing offense.

5. **Enhancing Job Satisfaction**: Let's face it—a workplace that's infused with humor is simply more enjoyable to be in. This can lead to higher job satisfaction among employees. When people are happy at work, they are more likely to stay with the company longer, hence reducing turnover rates. *Who doesn't want to stay in an environment where they can genuinely enjoy themselves?*

6. **Increasing Productivity**: You might think that humor would be distracting at work, but it's actually quite the opposite. Happy employees are productive employees. When people are in good spirits, they're more motivated and engaged with their tasks. I've noticed that teams with a good sense of humor tend to achieve their goals faster and more efficiently.

7. **On a personal level**: As an individual, humor makes you more approachable. Colleagues are more likely to come to you with ideas or problems if they feel comfortable around you. Leaders who use humor effectively also often find that it boosts team morale and loyalty. A happy team is a productive team!

8. **Conflict resolution:** And let's not forget conflict resolution; diffusing tense situations with a bit of well-placed humor can smooth things over faster than anything else.

Additionally, in meetings, humor can keep everyone engaged and make boring topics more interesting and hence, more effective.

BALANCING PROFESSIONALISM AND HUMOR

Showing up for your professional life is especially essential since our work life makes up a significant portion of our everyday life—to be specific, 5 days a week, approximately 40 hours. So, when it comes to the workplace, integrating humor with professionalism can significantly impact your environment positively. So, let's discuss how we can balance the two effectively:

1. Use Positive Humor

The first key to balancing professionalism and humor is to always aim for positive humor. This means avoiding jokes or comments that might come across as negative or offensive, just as you would in regular social settings. Positive humor uplifts people and can make a stressful day a bit lighter.

For instance, sharing a funny story about something innocuous or telling a light-hearted joke that everyone can relate to helps build camaraderie without crossing any boundaries. Positive humor doesn't target anyone or anything negatively; it focuses on finding joy in everyday situations.

For instance, during one particularly intense project at work, our team was feeling the strain. I decided to share a funny clip of a cat trying to catch a laser pointer during our break. It instantly lightened the mood and helped everyone relax a bit before diving back into the tasks at hand.

2. Encourage the Funny

Another effective way of balancing professionalism with humor is by creating space for others to share funny moments or jokes, especially if you are a leader. When done right, laughter can be incredibly contagious and provide a sense of unity within the team.

Fostering an environment where people feel safe to share their humorous stories or observations could be as simple as starting meetings with a *"funny moment of the week"* segment. Not only does this initiate meetings on a positive note, but it also provides team members with an opportunity to bond over shared laughter.

3. Don't Try to Be a Comedian

While it's great to incorporate humor into your professional life, it's essential not to try too hard or force it. Trying to be overly comedic can sometimes come off as insincere or inappropriate, which defeats the purpose of boosting morale.

Instead, let humor come naturally. You don't need to have a list of jokes ready — simply look for opportunities where you can share a laugh naturally throughout your day. Think about those moments where something funny happens spontaneously — those are often the best because they're genuine.

4. Read The Room

Being appropriate with your humor is crucial in maintaining professionalism. What might be funny in one context could be entirely inappropriate in another. Always consider your audience and the situation before making humorous comments.

For example, sarcasm may land well among close colleagues but could be misunderstood in client meetings or more formal settings. A big part of using humor professionally is simply knowing when and where it fits.

SITUATION	APPROPRIATE HUMOR
Team Meeting	Light-hearted jokes about daily work experiences
Client Presentation	Subtle humor related to industry trends (keeping it very professional)
Casual Office Chats	Funny personal anecdotes that are universally relatable (e.g., harmless pet stories)
Performance Reviews	Minimal humor — focus should remain professional but light wit can ease tension if used judiciously

5. Be Flexible

Lastly, being flexible with your approach is vital. Every workplace has its unique culture; what works in one place may not work in another due to different levels of formality or differing cultural norms regarding humor.

Use your self-awareness to pay attention to how others react to humor in your environment and adjust accordingly. If you find that certain types of jokes don't go over well, pivot towards what does resonate better within your team's culture.

Balancing professionalism and humor can make your work life more enjoyable and foster better relationships amongst colleagues. Always opt for positive humor; encourage others to bring their funny moments to the table, don't try too hard to be a comedian, be appropriate with your jokes, and stay flexible depending on your workplace culture.

WORKSHEET
Balancing Professionalism and Humor Reflect and Write

1. Think about a time when humor positively impacted a work situation for you. What happened? How did it improve the environment?

_____

_____

_____

_____

_____

_____

2. Recall a moment when humor was used inappropriately in your workplace. What was the outcome? How could it have been handled better?

_____

_____

_____

_____

_____

_____

3. Identify 3 ways you can incorporate positive humor into your daily work routine without compromising professionalism.

_____
_____
_____
_____
_____
_____
_____

4. List some types of humor that are universally appropriate in your workplace. How can you use these to build rapport with your colleagues?

_____
_____
_____
_____
_____
_____
_____

Self-Assessment

Think about recent situations at work where you used or witnessed humor. Rate yourself on the following (1 = never, 5 = always):

1. Using positive and uplifting humor:

☐1 ☐2 ☐3 ☐4 ☐5

2. Encouraging others to share funny moments:

☐1 ☐2 ☐3 ☐4 ☐5

3. Being natural with humor and not forcing it:

☐1 ☐2 ☐3 ☐4 ☐5

4. Ensuring humor is appropriate for the context:

☐1 ☐2 ☐3 ☐4 ☐5

5. Being flexible with humor based on setting:

☐1 ☐2 ☐3 ☐4 ☐5

Plan how you can improve in these areas if needed:

- Aim to identify opportunities throughout the day where a small joke or humorous comment feels right, rather than forcing it.
- Observe how colleagues respond to different types of humor and adjust accordingly.
- Keep a mental list of 'safe' topics for humor that are always appropriate, avoiding sensitive issues.
- Make an effort to balance levity with focus, ensuring that productivity is not compromised.

9

OVERCOMING CHALLENGES WITH HUMOR

―•••―

"A well-developed sense of humor is the pole that adds balance to your steps as you walk the tightrope of life."

~William Arthur Ward

Life has a funny way of throwing curveballs when we least expect them. Just when we think things are going smoothly, BAM! Something comes along to shake things up. It can be really challenging to maintain a positive outlook during such times. However, I've found that humor can be an incredible tool in navigating these rough patches. It might not fix the problem, but it changes how we feel about it and, as a result, how we deal with it.

One of the toughest periods I faced was when I lost my job unexpectedly. My immediate reaction was panic and sadness, of course. But after a while, I decided to find the humor in little things just to keep myself sane. I remember making up funny scenarios about what my former coworkers might be doing without me and imagining humorous ways I'd spend my newfound free time—like becoming a professional napper or starting a garden for pet rocks.

What surprised me the most was how humor helped me stay connected with others during this time. Whether face-to-face or through the phone, I'd share jokes and funny stories with friends and family and we'd end up laughing together. Don't get me wrong, this didn't instantly erase the stress, but it sure did create a sense of camaraderie and lighten the load.

Recently, I came across an interesting story about a woman named Karen who found herself facing a particularly tough year with back-to-back adversities ranging from a health scare to financial troubles. She decided to use humor as her coping mechanism. Every day, Karen wrote down something funny that happened or something that made her smile in her "Humor Journal." It turned into a daily ritual that not only lifted her spirits but became a treasure trove of happy moments she could revisit anytime she felt down.

Even in high-stress professions like healthcare, humor plays an especially vital role. Doctors and nurses often use humor as a coping strategy to keep spirits up. Simple pranks like putting googly eyes on medical equipment or sharing puns related to their field can make an otherwise somber situation more bearable.

Managing stress through humor isn't just anecdotal; there's some science backing it up too! An experiment involving two groups, where one used laughter therapy while facing stress, showed significant improvements in mood and coping ability compared to their non-laughing counterparts.

The good thing is, even when you are not able to connect with others for a good laugh, social media can bridge that gap. Platforms like TikTok and Instagram have become hotspots for quick laughs when facing personal challenges. People share their blunders, mishaps, and even their coping strategies through light-hearted content that often goes viral because it's relatable.

To visualize how we might incorporate humor into our lives during difficult times, here is a simple chart listing common situations where stress typically spikes and humorous activities that might help alleviate it:

Stressful Situation	Humorous Activity
Job Loss	Watch stand-up comedy/Imitate your favorite sketch
Relationship Problems	Share jokes or memes with friends
Financial Worries	Create funny budget cuts/mock newsletters
Health Concerns	Watch cheesy medical dramas/laugh at exaggerated plots
Family Discord	Play humorous board games/role-reversal scenarios
General Anxiety	Keep a humor journal/Follow funny social accounts

Using this chart as a guide can be your go-to reminder that where there's stress, there's also room for laughter.

FINDING JOY IN ADVERSITY

Over the years, I've faced my fair share of challenges, heartaches, and disappointments—as we all do. Sometimes, it felt easier to focus on the negative and let it consume me. But through various experiences, I realized that finding joy in adversity is not only possible but essential for our well-being.

One of the first steps to finding joy during difficult times is **shifting our mindset**. Instead of looking at a problem as insurmountable, try seeing it as an opportunity for growth. Early in my career in the U.S. Army, I found myself struggling through basic training, and thinking that I would be kicked out of the Army any day. The physical and mental parts of basic training were both so difficult for me that I could not envision success.

There were nights I cried myself to sleep, unsure of how I'd make it through. But everything began to change when I shifted my mindset and started viewing my situation through a more positive lens. The training didn't magically become easier, but my outlook made it feel more manageable and I began to excel. Looking back on my 20 years of service, I now realize that it was that shift in the way I viewed the challenges of basic training that laid the foundation for a successful and fulfilling military career.

Another important aspect is **building resilience**. Resilience isn't just about bouncing back; it's about bouncing forward with more strength and optimism than before. A tool that helped me immensely was practicing gratitude daily. Keeping a journal where I listed three things I was thankful for each day shifted my focus from what was going wrong to what was going right.

Here's a snippet from one week of my gratitude journal:

DAY	GRATEFUL FOR
MON	Morning coffee with a friend
TUE	The supportive call from my family
WED	The sound of rain while reading a favorite book
THU	A stranger's kind words

My gratitude journal continues:

DAY	GRATEFUL FOR
FRI	Discovering a new hobby - painting
SAT	A walk in the park
SUN	Reflective time and peace

Through consistency, this practice rewires our brain to seek out positivity and joy even in darker times.

Connecting with others is also essential in finding joy amid adversity. Human beings are innately social creatures, and having strong support systems can make a world of difference. During one particularly rough patch, involving the illness of a close family member, leaning on friends became paramount. We shared meals, stories, and laughter despite the challenging circumstances, creating moments of lightness and connection that carried us through.

It's also important to **recognize that small joys matter** just as much as big ones. Finding joy doesn't always involve monumental changes or achievements; sometimes it's in everyday moments—the aroma of freshly baked cookies, the first sip of coffee in the morning, or watching your favorite show after a long day.

Exercise and physical activity are another fantastic way to elevate mood and find happiness during hard times. When everything feels overwhelming, moving our bodies can be incredibly grounding. I started practicing yoga during depressive episodes and found it transformative, not just physically but mentally too.

Self-care shouldn't be overlooked either. It could be as simple as taking a quiet moment for yourself each day or engaging in hobbies that bring peace and contentment.

A vital lesson I've learned is **patience**—both with life's trials and with oneself. When facing adversity, it's easy to become impatient or self-critical if things aren't improving fast enough. But life isn't about instant gratification; it's about honoring each step forward, no matter how small.

Finding joy in adversity requires an openness—open eyes to see beyond immediate difficulties, an open heart to appreciate every positive fragment no matter how tiny, and an open mind ready for growth even from harsh experiences. It's really about cultivating a mindset that embraces life in all its complexity.

Just remember that joy doesn't mean ignoring pain, but finding ways to live alongside it without letting it overshadow our entire existence.

INSPIRING OTHERS WITH YOUR SENSE OF HUMOR

What if I told you that your sense of humor could inspire others and make a real difference in their lives? Let's discuss how you can use your light-heartedness to uplift the people around you.

Have you ever walked into a room filled with strangers and felt that uneasy tension hanging in the air? A well-timed, light-hearted joke can melt that tension away. It's like everyone collectively exhales, and suddenly, people feel more at ease. When people are comfortable, they are more **open to connecting**. This simple act of sharing a laugh breaks down walls and brings people closer together.

Another way your humor can inspire others is by **lifting their spirits** during tough times. Life is full of ups and downs, and sometimes we all need a little pick-me-up. When a friend is feeling blue, your funny anecdotes or silly impressions can be just what they need to see the lighter side of life again—laughter is contagious in the best of ways. By bringing joy into someone's life, you give them a momentary escape from their troubles and plant seeds of hope. They understand that joy is still possible, which can even make them more resilient.

So, how do you go about inspiring others with humor? It starts by being authentic. People can sense when you're being genuine or just trying too hard to be funny. Share the stories that make you laugh, the ones where things didn't go as planned but ended up being hilarious nonetheless. These genuine moments are relatable—we all have those quirky life experiences.

And remember, for humor to be effective, it needs to be used appropriately. If you need a refresher, refer back to Chapter 7 for some practical tips on how to do this.

Now, let's look at an example where humor can be deployed effectively:

Situation: A team meeting at work has become tense due to a looming project deadline.

Potential Response: *"I know it feels like we're trying to land a spaceship on Mars right now, but remember how we once tackled that huge project last year? And we didn't even need NASA's help!"*

A simple comment like this acknowledges the pressure but also lightens the mood by reminding everyone of past successes, with a humorous twist.

Another powerful way to use humor is through **storytelling**. Share those moments from your life that had everyone rolling on the floor laughing—whether it's an embarrassing childhood memory or a recent silly mishap at home. Stories draw people in and create connections because they illustrate shared human experiences.

PART III
BE OPTIMISTIC

10

UNDERSTANDING OPTIMISM

"Perpetual optimism is a force multiplier."

~Colin Powell

Optimism is more than just a sunny disposition. It's about having a hopeful and positive outlook on life, regardless of the challenges and hurdles that come our way. As an optimist, I tend to see the brighter side of things and believe that good things will happen, even when circumstances look bleak.

You might be wondering, *"Am I an optimist?"* Well, there are clear signs that can help us understand if we lean toward optimism. Optimistic people generally:

- Have a positive outlook on future events
- Focus on potential solutions rather than problems
- Can find silver linings even in difficult situations
- Have the ability to remain hopeful and resilient after experiencing setbacks. Optimists maintain their confidence and keep striving towards their goals.

Let's discuss the many benefits of embracing an optimistic outlook so that you can see the real magic of it:

1. **Better Health**: *Did you know that optimism is linked to better health outcomes?* That's right! Optimists tend to have lower rates of heart disease, reduced blood pressure, and even stronger immune systems. Think about it. When you're optimistic, you generally have a positive outlook on life, which reduces stress levels and promotes healthier lifestyle choices. For instance, you're more likely to exercise, eat well, and avoid overindulging in alcohol or other harmful substances.

2. **Emotional Health:** Optimism isn't just good for your physical health; it's beneficial for your emotional well-being too. Positive thinking can help combat feelings of anxiety and depression. When we expect good outcomes and focus on what's going right instead of dwelling on what's wrong, our overall mood improves. Imagine waking up each morning feeling hopeful about what the day holds rather than dreading potential pitfalls—who wouldn't want that?

3. **Greater Achievement**: Success often goes hand-in-hand with optimism. When we believe that good things will happen and that our efforts will pay off, we're more motivated to take action. This proactive approach often leads to better results. Optimists handle challenges as learning opportunities rather than discouraging setbacks—they actively seek solutions and come out stronger. I've found that in my own life, focusing on the possible positive outcomes rather than dwelling on potential failures has helped me in countless ways.

4. **Persistence:** Optimistic people are generally more resilient; they don't give up easily in the face of adversity. Instead of

seeing obstacles as dead ends, they see them as bumps in the road—a little frustrating maybe, but definitely passable. This mindset enables them to persevere where others might quit. Take Thomas Edison, for instance. We know that he failed over and over before finally inventing the light bulb. His optimistic outlook kept him persistent despite the numerous setbacks he faced.

5. **Increased Longevity:** *Do you want to live a longer life?* I know I do! Studies have shown that optimistic people tend to live longer than their pessimistic counterparts. Why? Well, it's likely due to a combination of all the factors we've already discussed: better health habits, lower stress levels, and improved emotional well-being all contribute to increased longevity.

Embracing optimism can transform our lives in remarkable ways, from improving our health and emotional well-being to achieving greater success and living longer lives without carrying the heavy burden of stress every day.

OPTIMISM VS. PESSIMISM

Have you ever noticed how some people always see the glass as half full while others always see it as half empty? That's essentially what optimism and pessimism are all about. And let me tell you, these perspectives can have a significant impact on our lives.

Optimists tend to look at the bright side of things. They believe that good things will happen in the future, and they tend to focus on the positives in any given situation. For example, if an optimist loses their job, they might think, *"Well, now I have a chance to find something even better."* This positive thinking can provide motivation and keep their spirits up in tough times.

Optimists often take action to improve their situations because they believe it will be worth it in the end. For example, they might be more inclined to set goals and work toward them, believing that success is achievable.

Now let's switch gears and take a look at pessimism. Pessimists often expect the worst outcome in any situation. They are naturally more inclined to focus on potential problems instead of solutions. If a pessimist loses their job, they might think, *"I'm never going to find another job like this one."* This outlook can lead to feelings of hopelessness and heightened anxiety.

But being a pessimist doesn't mean you're doomed to a miserable life. It's more complex than that. Some researchers argue that a little bit of pessimism can be helpful. For instance, defensive pessimism is a strategy where people lower their expectations to prepare for the worst possible outcomes. This way, if things do go wrong, they are not caught off guard and are better prepared mentally to handle setbacks.

Pessimists can also be more cautious decision-makers because they consider potential risks meticulously before taking action. This cautiousness can be beneficial in situations where too much optimistic risk-taking could lead to disaster.

Here's an interesting fact: it's not about being entirely one or the other—one can possess traits of both optimism and pessimism depending on different situations or stages in life.

ASPECT	OPTIMISM	PESSIMISM
Outlook	Sees the bright side; expects positive outcomes	Expects the worst outcomes
Reaction to setbacks	Motivated by challenges	Demoralized by challenges
Impact on health	Generally healthier and happier	Higher risk for depression and anxiety
Decision-making	Takes calculated risks	More cautious; considers risks closely

So, why does this matter in navigating life's journey? Here's why: your perspective—whether optimistic or pessimistic—can shape how you experience life itself. If you're naturally an optimist, fantastic! Use that sunny outlook to propel yourself forward, but remember not to become oblivious to potential risks; balance is key.

And if you lean towards pessimism? That's okay too! Use your cautious approach as a strength, but try also focusing on finding small positives amidst challenges—it might open up new avenues for growth you hadn't considered before.

Understanding where you fall on this spectrum can help tailor your strategies for dealing with life's ups and downs more effectively. **Here's a little exercise:** take a moment to think about your recent experiences or specific challenges you've faced. *Did you handle them with an optimistic outlook or a more pessimistic one? How did it impact the outcome?*

EMBRACING OPTIMISM THROUGH REAL-LIFE EXAMPLES

When I think of the powerful impact of optimism on our lives, two key figures come to mind. These examples epitomize how maintaining a positive outlook can turn even the bleakest circumstances into opportunities for personal growth and success.

J.K. Rowling

J.K. Rowling, the renowned author of the Harry Potter series, is a perfect example of how the power of optimism can change a life. Before she became a literary sensation, Rowling faced numerous hardships that would have deterred many others. She was a struggling single mother living on welfare and battling depression after a difficult separation from her husband.

Despite this, Rowling held onto her dream of becoming an author. She often spoke about the power of imagination and determination, which kept her going even on her darkest days. With the little money she had, she wrote much of Harry Potter and the Philosopher's Stone in various cafés around Edinburgh while her daughter slept beside her.

Rowling's firm belief in her story, combined with persistence, eventually paid off. After being rejected by twelve publishers, Bloomsbury finally accepted her manuscript. The rest is history; the Harry Potter series went on to become one of the best-selling book series of all time and catapulted Rowling to immense fame and success.

Her journey underscores an essential lesson: if you hold onto hope and persevere even when the odds feel stacked against you, great and incredible things can happen!

Malala Yousafzai

Malala Yousafzai's story is another great example of the strength that can be drawn from optimism in the face of adversity. Born in Pakistan's Swat Valley, Malala grew up advocating for girls' education amidst a regime that threatened such endeavors. Her passion for schooling was deeply inspired by her father, who ran a local school that welcomed children regardless of their family's financial ability.

At just 15 years old, Malala's advocacy made her a target for those opposing female education initiatives. In 2012, she survived an assassination attempt when a gunman shot her in the head while she was returning home on a school bus. The severity of her injuries required extensive medical treatment and rehabilitation in Birmingham, UK.

Despite this harrowing experience, Malala's spirit remained unbroken. Rather than retreating, she grew even more determined to fight for education rights worldwide, leading to the Malala Fund, which has helped—and continues helping—millions.

In 2014, at just 17 years old, Malala became the youngest-ever recipient of the Nobel Peace Prize. Her story showcases how optimism and resilience can fuel a transformation from victimhood to global leadership, inspiring countless others along the way.

LIFE CHALLENGE	OBSTACLE FACED	OPTIMISTIC ACTION TAKEN	RESULT
J.K. Rowling	Living on welfare; depression; rejections from publishers	Continued writing; persistent submissions	Became best-selling author
Malala Yousafzai	Shot by extremists; ongoing threats	Continued advocacy; founded Malala Fund	Nobel Peace Prize winner; global education advocate

These stories are reminders that optimistic thinking can be more than just wishful thoughts; it can be a profound power source leading us through adversity towards success and fulfillment.

WORKSHEET
Evaluating Your Level of Optimism

This worksheet is designed to help you evaluate your current level of optimism. Take some time to answer each question honestly. You can place your answers directly on the worksheet below or create a table with your responses.

1.When faced with a challenging situation, do you:

- Look for potential solutions (Yes/No)
- Focus on what went wrong (Yes/No)

2. How do you react to setbacks?

- See them as opportunities to learn and grow (Yes/No)
- Feel discouraged and defeated (Yes/No)

3. On most days, do you:

- Expect good things to happen (Yes/No)
- Worry about what might go wrong (Yes/No)

4. How do you interpret past negative experiences?

- As isolated events that don't define your future (Yes/No)
- As a pattern that will likely continue (Yes/No)

5. What's your outlook on your goals?

- Confident that you'll achieve them eventually (Yes/No)
- Doubtful about your ability to reach them (Yes/No)

6. When thinking about the future, do you:

- Feel hopeful and excited (Yes/No)
- Feel anxious and uncertain (Yes/No)

SCORING: Score yourself 1 point only for the "Yes" answers you gave yourself for the first bullet under each question. Calculate your total score.

MY TOTAL SCORE: _____

Interpreting Your Score:

- *5-6 points:* You are likely an optimist! Keep nurturing that positive outlook.

- *3-4 points:* You have a balanced perspective but might benefit from more optimistic thinking.
- *0-2 points:* You might lean more towards pessimism; consider focusing on building a more positive mindset.

Remember, the goal isn't to judge yourself at all, but to get an understanding of where you are and how you might improve. Embracing optimism is a journey, and each step counts toward creating a brighter future for yourself!

ACTION PLAN
Steps to Nurture an Optimistic Attitude

I've always believed that the key to unlocking happiness and success lies in a positive, can-do attitude. But let's be real—maintaining optimism isn't always a walk in the park. Life throws curveballs, and sometimes it feels like the world is conspiring against us. That's why having an actionable plan to nurture an optimistic attitude is so critical.

Here, I'll outline step-by-step what you can do to start making positivity your default setting:

STEP 1. 'Try On' a Positive Lens

Sometimes, our perspective colors everything we see. If you wore glasses with dirty lenses, everything would look grim and dull. Now, think about those same lenses but clean and clear; everything would appear much brighter. *'Trying on'* a positive lens means making the conscious decision to shift how we interpret the world around us.

The next time you face a challenge, pause and ask yourself how you can see this situation differently. *Is there a silver lining?* Perhaps it's an opportunity for growth or a lesson in resilience—either way, be keen enough to find out.

STEP 2. Take Note of the Company You Keep

Our social environment has a significant impact on our attitude. Spend time with people who lift you up, inspire you, and bring positivity into your life. Negative individuals can drain your energy and reinforce pessimistic views. Take a good look at your relationships and consider which ones make you feel good about yourself and your outlook on life, and which ones have the opposite effect. Surround yourself with optimistic people who encourage you to be your best self.

STEP 3. Turn Off the News

It's no secret that the news often focuses on negative events — disasters, conflicts, and crises (after all, that's what gets them the views). Consuming too much of this can skew your perception of the world and feed into a negative mindset.

While it's important to stay informed, it doesn't mean you should immerse yourself in negativity. Set limits on how much news you consume daily; maybe check updates once in the morning or evening, but not throughout the day. This way, you'll have more mental space for positive thoughts.

STEP 4. Write in a Journal for a Few Minutes Each Day

Journaling is also an effective tool for boosting your positivity as it allows you to reflect on your day thoughtfully. Spend a few minutes writing about what went well, what you're grateful for, or any positive experiences you had. Documenting these moments helps solidify them in your mind and encourages you to notice them more in the future.

Sample Journal Entry Template:

Date	Positive Experience	What I'm Grateful For
01-10	Achievement/Event	Person/Thing/Incident

By keeping these entries short and consistent, you'll create a powerful repository of positivity that you can revisit anytime.

STEP 5. Acknowledge What You Can — and Cannot — Control

One primary source of stress is focusing on things beyond our control. Identify what aspects of your life are within your control, such as your actions, reactions, and decisions, versus those that aren't — like other people's behavior or certain external events.

CAN CONTROL	CANNOT CONTROL
My effort in tasks	The outcome of those tasks
How I respond to situations	Other people's opinions
Decisions I make	External factors, e.g., the weather

Directing energy towards what you can control empowers you, while letting go of uncontrollable factors frees you and reduces unnecessary anxiety.

STEP 6. Don't Forget to Acknowledge the Negative

Negative feelings or situations are a natural part of life, and pretending they don't exist won't make them disappear. Instead, acknowledge these moments without letting them dominate your mindset. Accepting negativity as part of life helps balance your perspective rather than denying or burying those experiences.

For instance:

- When dealing with disappointment, allow yourself to feel sad momentarily, but then focus on what steps you can take next.
- If you're feeling anxious about something outside of your control (recalling step 5), acknowledge that anxiety before shifting focus on actionable steps within your realm.

STEP 7. Practice Acts of Kindness

Kindness is a simple yet powerful way to boost your own optimism. When you do something kind for someone else, it creates a ripple effect of positivity. It doesn't have to be anything grand—small acts can make a big difference.

For instance, you can hold the door open for someone, send a thoughtful message to a friend, or even volunteer for a cause you care about. The joy and satisfaction from such acts help reinforce a positive mindset in both you and the people around you.

STEP 8. Have a Solid Morning Routine

How you start your day sets the tone for the rest of it. Incorporate positive practices into your morning routine to help launch you into the day with an optimistic mindset.

Some things to consider:

    a. *Exercise:* Physical activity releases endorphins, which make you feel good.

    b. *Meditation or Mindfulness:* Spending just five minutes centering yourself can significantly impact your outlook.

    c. *Reading or Listening to Something Inspirational:* Start your day with words that uplift and inspire.

STEP 9. Set Small, Achievable Goals

Setting and achieving small goals can create a sense of accomplishment and forward momentum. These goals don't have to be monumental—small steps add up over time and can significantly impact your overall optimism.

For example, aim to read one chapter of a book per week, take a short daily walk, or learn a new skill in small increments. As you achieve these goals, you'll build confidence and optimism towards setting and tackling bigger aspirations.

STEP 10. Celebrate Your Wins

Big or small, every achievement deserves recognition. Celebrating your successes fosters an optimistic attitude by reminding you of what you've accomplished. It provides motivation to keep moving forward. Create a "***wins***" journal where you jot down daily or weekly accomplishments. Reflect on these victories regularly; they serve as tangible evidence of your progress and reinforce positivity.

As you follow these steps consistently, you'll find that being optimistic becomes second nature, and this attitude will empower you across all areas of your life. Remember, nurturing optimism is an ongoing process—each step counts towards creating a more positive outlook daily.

11

DEVELOPING AN OPTIMISTIC ATTITUDE

―••●••―

"Optimism is the faith that leads to achievement; nothing can be done without hope."

~Helen Keller

Have you ever noticed how, when you're in a good mood and think positively, things just seem to work out better? Optimism opens doors to opportunities. When you believe in good outcomes, you're more likely to take risks and try new things.

This proactive approach often leads to personal and professional growth. And as we've seen, an optimistic attitude doesn't simply make us happier; it also significantly improves our physical health, relationships, and overall quality of life.

CHANGING NEGATIVE THOUGHT PATTERNS

We all have those moments when negative thoughts just seem to take over. These moments can form a repetitive pattern of subconscious beliefs or attitudes that lean toward the pessimistic side. They could be anything from *"I'm not good enough"* to *"This will never work."* The problem with these thoughts is that they can become so ingrained in us that they start affecting our behavior, decisions, and overall happiness.

But the good news is that you have the power to change these negative thought patterns. Sure, it's not going to happen overnight, but with some consistent effort, you can certainly overcome them.

1. Identify Areas to Change: The first step towards a more positive mindset is identifying which areas of your life are dominated by negativity. *Is it your work, health, relationships, or even your self-worth?* For instance, I noticed that every time I faced a challenge at work, my initial thought was always that I wasn't good enough. Identifying this helped me focus on where I needed to change.

Note: It can be helpful to keep a journal or a simple notebook where you write down when these negative thoughts occur and what triggers them.

2. Check Yourself: Once you've identified your negative thought patterns, it's important to check yourself regularly. When you catch yourself thinking negatively, pause and analyze why this thought surfaced.

For example:

SITUATION	NEGATIVE THOUGHT	RATIONAL RESPONSE
Failed at a task	"I'm such a failure."	"This was one task; it doesn't define my entire ability."
Argued with a friend	"They must hate me now."	"We just had a disagreement; it doesn't mean we're not friends anymore."

Checking yourself helps you understand and challenge your negative thoughts logically.

3. Be Open to Humor: As we saw in our previous section on humor, laughter really is the best medicine! Sometimes when we're stuck in a cycle of negative thinking, we forget how to smile or laugh. Surrounding myself with humor—whether through funny movies, jokes from friends, or even humorous books—has pulled me out of many dark clouds.

One time, I was feeling particularly down about missing out on an opportunity at work, and my friend sent me a hilarious meme about office life. It made me laugh so hard that the sting of that missed opportunity faded away significantly.

4. Adopt a Healthy Lifestyle: Our physical health greatly affects our mental state. Engaging in regular exercise, maintaining a nutritious diet, and getting enough sleep can drastically improve our mood and energy levels. I've made it a habit to go for daily walks, which not only keep me fit but also give me time to clear my mind and embrace positivity.

Here's a simple routine that I follow to maintain a healthy lifestyle, no matter what the day brings. Feel free to tweak it to suit your needs, and don't forget to establish solid eating and exercise habits too.

Morning: I start with stretching or yoga for 15 minutes, whether I exercise that day or not.

Afternoon: I always make sure to eat a balanced lunch with plenty of veggies and lean protein for sustained energy for the last half of the day. This is especially important if your mornings are hectic and you've only managed to grab a coffee and a pastry—quick fixes that won't carry you far.

Evening: I like to wind down with light activities like walking or cycling—great for keeping fit and perfect for relaxation.

Surround Yourself with Positive People: Just as we mentioned that our social connections are essential for maintaining an optimistic outlook, the company we keep can directly contribute to a negative/positive mindset.

Take stock: Are the people around you supportive and positive? If not, it might be time to distance yourself from those who bring negativity into your life.

I once had to distance myself from someone who constantly criticized everything I did, which took a toll on my mental and emotional well-being. Instead, I started spending more time with friends who uplifted me and believed in my potential. This shift made an enormous difference in my outlook on life.

5. Practice Positive Self-Talk: Finally, positive self-talk can transform how you view yourself and the world around you. Instead of berating yourself for mistakes or shortcomings, practice speaking kindly to yourself. A simple way to do this is by replacing negative thoughts with positive affirmations. Reinforcing positive thoughts will help shift your mindset over time.

For example:

NEGATIVE THOUGHT	POSITIVE SELF-TALK
"I'll never get this right."	"I'm learning and improving bit by bit."
"I can't do this."	"I can handle this, one step at a time."
"I'm not worthy."	"I am enough just as I am."

6. Learn from Mistakes: Instead of viewing mistakes as failures, view them for what they really are: learning opportunities. Each mistake teaches us something valuable and helps us grow. Reflect on what went wrong, what you learned from the situation, and how you can improve in the future.

There was a time I completely flopped when presenting an idea at work. Instead of letting it bring me down, I took a step back and tried to figure out what went wrong. With this knowledge, I practiced more for my next presentation. This not only improved my skill but also boosted my confidence the next time I stood up to speak.

Avoid dwelling on the past or worrying excessively about the future—remember that you can't do much to change either. But staying in the present and acting in the now is what brings real change and can help you maintain a positive outlook. Mindfulness techniques such as meditation can be very effective in keeping us grounded and focused on the present moment.

These strategies might seem simple, but their combined effect is truly life-changing. In my journey toward an optimistic outlook, each step has built upon the last, creating an upward spiral of positivity.

So, if you're tired of being bogged down by negative thoughts and are ready for a change, give these tips a try! Start small by focusing on one area at first instead of everything all at once. Gradually integrate these strategies into your daily routine until they become habits.

GRATITUDE PRACTICES

We've touched a little on gratitude in the previous chapters, but when it comes to changing negative thought patterns, this practice is indispensable. Gratitude goes much deeper than just saying *"thank you"* when someone holds the door open for you. It's about appreciating the good things in your life, big or small. It's looking at your everyday experiences through a lens of thankfulness and recognizing all the positives that come your way.

Besides gratitude journaling, which we have covered several times before, below are some tips and practices that have worked wonders for me, and I believe they'll do the same for you:

1. Practice Mindful Appreciation: We often rush through our days without stopping to appreciate the world around us. Take a moment each day to practice mindful appreciation. This means being fully present and noticing the small details around you— whether it's the weight of your coffee mug in your hand, the buzzing of the photocopy machine at work, or simply your footsteps hitting the ground during your evening walk. Stay in the moment and take it all in.

2. Voice Your Gratitude: Don't keep all that positive energy bottled up! Make it a point to express your gratitude to others. Tell your coworker you appreciate their help with that project, or let your family know how much their support means to you. Bringing these feelings into the open not only lifts others up but also reinforces your own sense of thankfulness.

3. Create Gratitude Rituals: Incorporate gratitude into your daily routines with small rituals. For instance, during meals, take a moment before eating to silently express thanks for the food in front of you and everyone who made it possible, from the farmers to the cooks and anyone else in between.

A simple routine like this can make everyday experiences more meaningful:

TIME	ROUTINE EXAMPLE
Morning	Take two minutes to reflect on what you're grateful for today
Meal Time	Say thanks before each meal
Evening	Write in your gratitude journal

4. Reflect on Challenges as Opportunities: It might sound counterintuitive, but try being grateful for challenges too. They offer valuable lessons and opportunities for growth, even if it's hard to see it at first glance. By reframing obstacles as opportunities, you're training yourself to look for the silver lining in difficult situations.

5. Share Stories of Gratitude: There is something incredibly powerful about sharing stories of gratitude with others. Whether it's during a family dinner, a gathering with friends, or even on social media, talking about what you're thankful for can spread positivity both within and without.

6. Use Visual Reminders: Sometimes we need little nudges throughout the day to remind us to practice gratitude. Sticky notes with positive messages around your home or workspace would work great. You can write things like *"Be thankful," "Look for the good,"* or *"Appreciate what you have."* Every time you see one, take a moment to reflect on something you're grateful for.

7. Join a Gratitude Group: Sometimes it helps to connect with others who have the same goals as you do — in this case, being more grateful. Look for online communities or local groups that meet to discuss and share gratitude practices. Here are sample search phrases that can yield good results: *Gratitude community near me, gratitude groups Facebook,* or *gratitude club.*

MY CHECKLIST FOR DEVELOPING AN ATTITUDE OF GRATITUDE	
PRACTICE	FREQUENCY
Keep a Gratitude Journal	Daily
Practice Mindful Appreciation	Daily
Voice Your Gratitude	Daily
Create Gratitude Rituals	Daily
Reflect on Challenges	As needed
Share Stories of Gratitude	Weekly
Use Visual Reminders	Always
Join a Gratitude Group	Monthly

Incorporating these practices into your daily life is a great way to build a more optimistic attitude. Just remember, it's the small things you do consistently that make all the difference.

VISUALIZATION TECHNIQUES

Visualization is a focused and deliberate use of your mind to picture specific scenarios or outcomes—and no, it's not simply daydreaming. Think of it as creating a mental rehearsal for success. As you visualize, you trick your brain into thinking that what you're imagining has already happened or is on its way to happening. Numerous studies have shown that when we visualize something vividly and repeatedly, our brain starts to create new neural pathways, making the imagined scenarios seem more achievable, which can prompt us into action.

So, why is visualization so important, especially when it comes to developing an optimistic attitude? Well, our brains are wired to focus on what's familiar. This means that if you constantly visualize positive outcomes, your mind will start recognizing such scenarios as normal and expected. Over time, this habit can shift your mindset from one of doubt and negativity to one of possibility and confidence.

Here are some types of visualizations that you can try out:

1. The Perfect Day Visualization: What would a perfect day look like for you? Imagine this, starting from the moment you wake up and spell out every small detail until you go to bed at night. Visualize yourself feeling happy, productive, and satisfied throughout the day. Think about the people you interact with, the things you do, and how you feel in each moment. The aim is to immerse yourself fully in this imagined scenario.

When I do this exercise, I picture myself waking up refreshed, having a healthy breakfast, and going about my day feeling confident and efficient. This mental imagery helps set a positive tone for my actual day.

2. Gratitude Visualization: We've talked a lot about gratitude journaling, *but have you ever tried visualizing gratitude?* Close your eyes and visualize three things you're thankful for. Picture them vividly and let yourself feel the warmth of those blessings.

For instance, I often visualize my family's smiles, my home office where creativity flows freely, and nature's beauty during my morning walks. This practice instantly lifts my mood and aligns me with positivity.

3. Vision Board Exercise: Here, you create a vision board, but using mental imagery instead of physical pictures. Close your eyes and "*pin*" images that represent your goals—career achievements, health milestones, happy relationships—onto this imaginary board.

I often "*place*" images of new book launches, speaking engagements with enthusiastic audiences, and family vacations into my mental vision board. Each time I close my eyes to review this board, I feel motivated and one step closer to achieving these goals.

4. Future Self Visualization: This is one of my favorites! Take some time to envision yourself five or ten years from now living your best life. *Where are you? What are you doing? How have you grown?*

Whenever I do this exercise, I see myself thriving in personal and professional spheres—cultivating deeper relationships, being more knowledgeable, and physically fit. This not only paints a bright future but also guides my present actions towards these aspirations.

5. Positive Affirmations Visualization: You can pair positive affirmations with visualization for greater impact! For each affirmation you say out loud or think silently, create a matching mental image. For example:

- Affirmation: "I am confident."
- Visualization: Picture yourself speaking confidently in meetings.
- Affirmation: *"I attract abundance."*
- Visualization: See opportunities knocking on your door (make sure it's specific, e.g., your desired bank account balance, or securing your dream job).

Combining words with vivid pictures embeds these affirmations deeper into your subconscious mind.

6. Relaxation Visualization: Visualization can also help us wind down. Incorporate visualization into your relaxation routine by imagining serene environments—it could be a beach sunset or a peaceful forest trail. What's your idea of serene? Think about it and allow every detail to wash over you as if you're truly there.

When stress hits me hard, I imagine sitting by calmer waters watching the waves gently lap onto shore under a golden twilight—nothing but pure tranquility filling my senses.

7. Morning Intention Setting: A fantastic way to start your day on a positive note is by setting clear intentions in the morning. Before beginning the day's activities, take a moment to sit quietly and decide what kind of day you want to have. Visualize the most important tasks you'll tackle, the mindset you want to maintain, and the positive interactions you'll have.

For example, I often set intentions such as being productive at work, expressing gratitude throughout the day, and staying calm in challenging situations. Visualizing these scenarios helps me mentally prepare myself to follow through with these intentions.

Remember, practice makes perfect! The more regularly you incorporate these visualization techniques into your routine, the more naturally optimistic you'll become in your day-to-day life.

12

OPTIMISM IN ACTION

―•••―

"Few things in the world are more powerful than a positive push. A smile. A world of optimism and hope. A 'you can do it' when things are tough."

~Richard M. DeVos

Practicing optimism means taking an active approach to life's challenges, powered by a positive mindset and deliberate, concrete action. Taking this optimistic approach doesn't imply that you ignore challenges or be unrealistically cheerful; instead, it's all about facing setbacks with resilience and finding ways to move forward despite obstacles. It's not enough to merely feel hopeful; we must be able to translate that hope into tangible actions that drive us forward. This approach is important because it ensures that our positive mindset yields real-world results.

Optimism gives us the energy and enthusiasm to pursue our dreams. When we believe that good things are possible, we're more likely to set our sights high and take the necessary steps to see our goals through. Without this positive outlook, it's easy to get bogged down by doubts and fears that usually hold us back.

SETTING AND ACHIEVING POSITIVE GOALS

Goals are essentially our desired outcomes for the future—they can range from short-term objectives like finishing a project at work to long-term dreams such as writing a novel or running a marathon. Either way, they provide direction, keeping us focused on where we want to go.

Positive goals are tied to positive acts, thoughts, and feelings. These are goals that not only achieve something valuable but also make you feel accomplished and happy. Take a moment to think about it: when you set goals that genuinely align with your values and desires, you're more motivated to work towards them.

For instance:

NEGATIVE GOAL	POSITIVE GOAL
Lose Weight	Get Fit and Healthy (positive focus)
Quit Procrastinating	Start Managing Time Better (positive)
Avoid Debt	Build Financial Security (positive)

STEPS TO SET POSITIVE GOALS

Here's a simple step-by-step process for setting positive (and actionable) goals:

1. Identify Your Values and Priorities: The first step in setting positive goals is to understand what truly matters to you. Ask yourself: *What do I value most in life? What makes me happy?* Write all your values down and ensure you prioritize them in any goals you set moving forward. Knowing your values helps you set goals that are meaningful and motivating.

2. Be Specific: When setting a goal, it's important to be as specific as possible. If you say, *"I want to be healthier,"* this is a great sentiment, but it can be hard to act on. Try something more concrete, like *"I want to walk 30 minutes every day."* Specific goals give you a clear target to aim for and also make it easier to track progress.

3. Make Your Goals Measurable: A good goal is one that you can measure. Such a goal allows you to see how far you've come and how much further you need to go. If your goal is to save money, determine the exact amount you want to save, such as *"I want to save $500 in three months."*

4. Set Achievable Goals: While it's great to chase big dreams, it's important that your first steps are within reach. For instance, if you're new to running and want to run a marathon, don't aim for it right away.

Start with a 5K run, tick that off, aim for a 7K, 10K, until you get to the marathon. Setting gradual, achievable goals helps maintain motivation and momentum by providing attainable milestones along the way.

5. Ensure Relevance: Goals stick when they matter to you. Your goals should align with your values and long-term objectives. Setting relevant goals means they should matter to you and contribute positively toward your bigger vision for life.

6. Commit to a Time Frame: Setting deadlines for your goals adds a sense of urgency and helps you prioritize tasks effectively. Whether short-term or long-term, having a time frame keeps you focused on making consistent progress.

7. Create an Action Plan: An action plan outlines the steps necessary to achieve your goal. Break down the overall goal into smaller tasks or milestones that can be completed step-by-step.

For instance:

GOAL	STEPS	TIMELINE
Save $500 in 3 months	Create a budget	1 week
	Open a savings account	1 week
	Save $40 each week	Weekly
Walk 30 minutes daily	Get walking shoes	2 days
	Schedule time for walks	1 day
	Track daily walk time	Daily

Life is unpredictable, so it's essential to remain flexible with your plans without losing sight of the end goal. If obstacles arise, adjust your action plan accordingly, but keep moving forward.

STAYING MOTIVATED DURING SETBACKS

We've all faced setbacks at some point in our lives. Whether it's a failed project, a missed opportunity, or a personal disappointment, setbacks can be disheartening. But here's the thing—it's not the setback itself that defines us; it's how we respond to it. Staying motivated during setbacks can be challenging, but it's entirely possible with the right mindset and strategies.

So, how do you stay motivated?

1. **Take It Bit By Bit:** One thing that always helps me stay motivated during tough times is setting small, achievable goals. When I was working on a big project last year and things weren't going as planned, I felt overwhelmed and demotivated. Instead of focusing on the entire project, I broke it down into smaller tasks and celebrated each little victory. These small successes kept me going and eventually led to the successful completion of the project.

2. **Befriend Your Inner Self:** Another important factor in staying motivated is maintaining a positive inner dialogue. Our thoughts have a powerful impact on our emotions and actions. Whenever I catch myself thinking negatively or doubting myself, I consciously replace those thoughts with positive affirmations. It might sound simplistic, but telling myself *"I can do this"* or *"This setback is temporary"* genuinely lifts my spirits and pushes me forward.

3. **Have A Solid Support System:** Connecting with supportive people who can offer encouragement and advice during times of setbacks is crucial. I've found that talking about my struggles often brings new perspectives and solutions that I hadn't considered before. Your friends or family can also provide much-needed emotional support.

4. **Look Back:** Reflecting on past achievements is another way to boost motivation during difficult times. Whenever I'm feeling down about a current setback, I look back at challenges I've overcome in the past. Remembering that I've

successfully navigated tough situations before gives me confidence that I can do it again.

5. **Blow Off Steam:** Exercise is another powerful tool for maintaining motivation. As we saw earlier, physical activity is known to release endorphins, which naturally improve mood and energy levels. Whenever I'm stuck in a rut, going for a run or even just taking a walk clears my mind and revitalizes my spirit.

6. **Slow Down:** Pushing yourself after a setback can feel productive, but if we are real, it's only a shortcut to burnout and further demotivation. Allowing yourself to take breaks can prevent this, recharge you, and keep your motivation levels high—this is perfect for maintaining productivity over the long haul.

Remember, it's not about avoiding setbacks altogether—because they're inevitable—but about showing up every day with an optimistic attitude and actionable plan to navigate through them. With persistence and the right approach, you can turn setbacks into stepping stones towards your success.

CELEBRATING SMALL WINS

Life is a series of ups and downs, but it's the little victories that light up our journey. Celebrating small wins may sound trivial to some, but trust me, it's more powerful than you might think. It's like fueling your car for a long trip; those small pit stops keep the engine running and you moving forward.

One time, I was juggling multiple projects at work while trying to stay on top of my personal commitments. It felt overwhelming.

Every day seemed like an uphill battle, and the big goals I had set for myself seemed out of reach. One morning, as I was sipping my coffee, it hit me—why not celebrate the tiny milestones? So, I started a simple ritual every day. I'd jot down three small achievements in my journal before going to bed. They could be as minor as clearing out my email inbox or having a good conversation with a colleague.

It felt almost magical. Those little acknowledgments of progress brought a wave of positivity and motivation into my life. And that's the essence of celebrating small wins—boosting your morale one step at a time.

According to Harvard Business Review, Teresa Amabile and Steven Kramer coined the term *"The Progress Principle."* They found that tracking small achievements each day enhances inner work life and boosts long-term success. When you recognize a small win, your brain releases dopamine, which makes you feel good and encourages you to keep pushing forward. It's like giving yourself a high-five for moving closer to your goals.

HOW TO CELEBRATE SMALL WINS

1. **Create a Daily Routine:** Start by allocating just five minutes each day to acknowledge your minor victories. Write them down in a journal or make mental notes.

2. **Share Your Wins:** Share your accomplishments with friends or family members who support and care for you. A small cheer from loved ones can amplify your joy.

3. **Visual Reminders:** Use sticky notes or digital reminders on your phone or laptop. Every time you see them, you'll get a boost, remembering that you're making progress.

4. **Reward Yourself:** Treat yourself to something enjoyable — your favorite cheat meal, an episode of your favorite show/podcast, or even some quiet time with a book.

5. **Reflect Periodically:** At the end of each week or month, look back at all the small wins you've written down. This can be incredibly uplifting and affirming.

Personal Growth Through Micro-Achievements

As I nurtured my new habit of celebrating small wins, I started growing in ways I never imagined possible through such a small act. All these small accomplishments served as building blocks, gradually contributing to my overall development and self-improvement.

For example, one of my goals was to become a more effective communicator. Instead of aiming to give a flawless presentation right away, I celebrated smaller milestones like effectively conveying a point during a meeting or receiving positive feedback from a colleague. These mini-successes made me more confident and gradually improved my public speaking skills.

Celebrating small wins isn't strictly about work. It can apply to all areas of life — whether it's sticking to a workout routine, cooking a healthy meal, or even maintaining relationships by reaching out to friends. Every small success counts and brings you closer to your larger aspirations.

Here's a simple worksheet you can use to keep track of your micro-achievements:

DATE	SMALL WIN	HOW IT MADE ME FEEL

Try to fill this out at the end of each day, writing down any small win you experience, no matter how insignificant it may seem. Then reflect on how that win made you feel. This daily practice can significantly uplift your spirits and keep you motivated.

13

INFLUENCING OTHERS WITH OPTIMISM

―――・●●・―――

"Try to be a rainbow in someone else's cloud."

~Maya Angelou

One of the most powerful, life-changing tools that we all have is the ability to influence others. And when we do this with optimism, the results can be pretty incredible. Showing up with a positive attitude not only helps us but also encourages, inspires, and uplifts those around us—and in this chapter, we will see how.

Let me start with a simple truth I've learned: **positivity is contagious**. When you approach situations with a hopeful outlook, it sets the tone for everyone involved. Whether you're at work, at home, or just meeting new people, your optimistic demeanor can create a ripple effect. People tend to mirror the energy of those around them. So, if you show up with enthusiasm and confidence, others are more likely to feel and act the same way.

However, just like cultivating optimism within yourself, influencing others with it isn't about ignoring problems or pretending everything is perfect. It's about facing challenges head-on with a belief that solutions are possible. When people see that you acknowledge difficulties but remain hopeful about overcoming them, they are more inclined to trust and follow your lead.

Take group projects, for instance. I've seen firsthand that teams led by optimistic leaders generally perform better and have higher morale than those led by pessimistic ones. The reason? An optimistic leader doesn't shy away from problems but instead motivates the team by focusing on possibilities and solutions rather than obstacles. This outlook encourages creativity and resilience within the group.

Now, let's dive into some practical ways to influence others using optimism:

1. **Express Genuine Interest:** When talking to someone, genuinely listen and show interest in what they have to say. This gives them a sense of being important and valued, which can boost their mood and outlook.

2. **Share Success Stories:** Sharing stories of success and overcoming adversity can inspire and motivate others. These stories act as proof that challenges can be overcome, providing hope during tough times. Just make sure the stories you share are relevant to the context, and be mindful of your tone—you don't want to come across as bragging, as that could have the opposite effect of what you intended.

3. **Offer Encouragement:** Simple words of encouragement like *"You can do this"* or *"I believe in you"* go a long way in boosting someone's confidence and motivating them.

4. **Practice Gratitude:** Showing gratitude for even the small things helps create a positive atmosphere around you. By

acknowledging good in others and situations, you teach those around you to do the same.

5. **Lead by Example:** People are more likely to be optimistic if they see it in action. In tough times, maintain your positive attitude and demonstrate problem-solving behaviors.

6. **Use Positive Language:** The words we choose have power over our mindset as well as that of others. Using positive language helps shift the perspective from problems to opportunities.

Real Life Examples

Professional setting: Let's say you are at work, where stress levels are high due to an upcoming deadline. As an optimistic person leading your team or simply being part of it, you could say something like: *"Remember when we faced that last project challenge? We nailed it because we focused on what we could control and supported each other throughout."* This reminder highlights past successes while instilling faith in collective capability.

Personal setting: At home, if someone is struggling with personal issues, offering words of encouragement like, *"I know it's tough right now, but I believe in your strength and ability to get through this,"* can uplift their spirit.

Social and community settings: By expressing genuine interest in conversations and actively listening in social gatherings, you make others feel valued and heard. This can enhance your relationships and help you nurture a supportive network. In community events, practicing gratitude can have a remarkable effect. For example, acknowledging the efforts of volunteers by saying, *"Your dedication makes such a positive impact on our community,"* fosters a sense of appreciation and belonging.

Here is a breakdown of how you can instill optimism in others in different settings:

SETTING	ACTION	RESULT
Work	Share success stories	Colleagues feel motivated
Home	Offer encouragement	Family members' confidence increases
Social Gatherings	Express genuine interest	Enhances relationships
Community Events	Practice gratitude	Creates a positive community vibe

By incorporating these practical ways into our daily lives, we not only uplift those around us but also reinforce our own optimistic perspective.

CREATING A POSITIVE COMMUNITY

Whether it's in your neighborhood, at work, or even online, creating an environment where everyone feels welcomed and supported can make a significant difference in our daily lives. In this section, I'm going to share some practical ways we can all contribute to making our communities more positive:

1. Communication: This is the backbone of any thriving community. We need to be open and honest with one another. Listen more than you speak, and when you do speak, make sure you're clear and kind. Communication isn't just about talking; it's also about understanding each other.

I've found that when everyone feels heard, they're more likely to contribute positively. We can practice good communication by holding regular meetings, whether they're in person or virtual. This helps everyone stay on the same page and gives people a chance to voice their thoughts and concerns.

2. Inclusivity: A positive community welcomes everyone with open arms. Let's embrace diversity in all its forms—cultural, racial, gender, age...you name it. An inclusive environment allows each member to feel valued, respected, and that they belong.

One way to promote inclusivity is by celebrating different cultures or simply learning about each other's backgrounds. This brings us closer and allows for deeper connections.

3. Participation: Participation is key to making a community vibrant and active. Encourage everyone to take part in activities and decisions. If you're planning an event or making a decision that impacts the group, getting input from as many members as possible ensures that everyone has a stake in the outcome.

Sometimes people might feel shy or hesitant to participate; this is where friendly encouragement comes in handy. Create opportunities where even those who are typically quiet feel comfortable sharing their ideas.

4. Conflict Resolution: No community is immune to conflicts, but it's how we handle them that counts. Address issues as soon as they arise with patience and empathy. Avoid blame games; instead, focus on finding solutions together. It also helps to have some ground rules for resolving conflicts, like active listening and speaking calmly, which can guide you through the tough spots without causing lasting damage.

CONFLICT TYPE	RECOMMENDED APPROACH
Miscommunication	Clarify & Confirm Understandings
Personal Differences	Empathy & Mediation
Resource Allocation	Negotiation & Fair Distribution

5. Supportive Environment: A positive community is also a supportive one. Be there for one another during good times and bad. Celebrate achievements together and provide comfort during difficulties. Creating this supportive environment involves acts both big and small—from organizing meal trains for someone going through a rough patch to simply lending an ear when someone needs to talk.

6. Shared Goals or Values: Communities flourish best when their members share common goals or values. These could be anything from promoting local art scenes to creating sustainable living practices. These shared aims give you purpose and direction, making it easier for everyone to pull together towards something meaningful.

7. Environmental Consideration: Today, being mindful of our environmental impact is a necessity. A positive community should think green! Here, you can organize carpool programs, recycling drives, or community gardens. Not only does this help our planet, but it also brings us closer as we work towards a common cause.

Plus, nature activities like hikes or picnics are excellent ways to bond while appreciating the environment around us.

8. Fun Activities: Activities that bring joy help maintain morale and create memorable experiences that reinforce bonds within your community. Organizing game nights, talent shows, or even simple picnics can provide relaxed settings for people to connect on a personal level outside of regular routines or responsibilities. These activities not only provide a break from the routine but also give us a chance to connect on a more personal level.

These elements will help build stronger connections and make your community a nurturing space for everyone involved. It's all about showing up for each other and creating a space where everyone feels welcome, heard, and valued. Let's get out there and start making our communities the best they can be!

THE RIPPLE EFFECT OF POSITIVE THINKING

If you toss a pebble into still water, the ripples spread out far and wide. Positive thinking works the same; it starts small, but the effects can touch every aspect of our lives.

1. Health and Wellness

One of the most fascinating aspects of positive thinking is how it influences our health. Studies have shown that maintaining a positive outlook can actually lower your risk of heart disease. Imagine that! Also, a positive mind often leads to healthier behaviors, like regular exercise and better eating habits, which all contribute to overall well-being.

Additionally, our immune systems respond to positive thinking! It's incredible how our bodies and minds are so interconnected. A study found that people who practiced optimism had stronger immune responses when compared to those who didn't maintain an optimistic outlook.

Physical health isn't the only area influenced by a positive mindset. It also impacts mental health in significant ways. When we think positively, we're more resilient to stress and better able to cope with life's challenges. It's like building a mental toolkit filled with resources to face whatever comes our way. Positive thinkers are less likely to suffer from depression and anxiety because they have an inner belief that things will get better.

2. Better Relationships

But the impact doesn't stop with ourselves; it extends to our relationships with others. Have you ever noticed that when you're around someone who is consistently upbeat and encouraging, it lifts your spirits? Positive thinkers tend to attract people who share similar outlooks, creating an uplifting social circle where everyone benefits.

3. Productivity

People who engage in positive thinking often find themselves more productive in life. When you believe in your abilities and maintain a hopeful attitude, you're more likely to set goals and follow through on them.

Positive thoughts lead to positive actions, which often result in successful outcomes.

4. General Contentment

In terms of achieving goals and life satisfaction, maintaining a positive mindset plays a critical role. When we set goals with a positive attitude, we're more likely to approach them methodically and enthusiastically. This enthusiasm fuels perseverance, making us more determined not just to start tasks but also to see them through to completion.

5. Collective Effect

Community involvement highlights another layer of this ripple effect. Positive thinkers who engage with their communities often inspire others around them, leading to collective improvement and better communal bonds. It's no exaggeration to say that one person's positive attitude can catalyze change within their entire neighborhood or community group.

It's also worth noting that organizations have started recognizing this ripple effect in their corporate wellness programs. Companies promoting positivity see enhanced morale among employees leading to reduced turnover rates and higher job satisfaction.

To give a structured view of these impacts:

AREAS AFFECTED	SPECIFIC OUTCOMES
Physical Health	Lower risk of heart disease; healthier habits
Mental Health	Reduced stress; increased resilience; decreased risk of depression
Relationships	Improved social connections; attracts supportive peers

Productivity	Enhanced goal-setting; higher achievement rates
Immune System	Stronger immune responses
Goal Achievement	Higher motivation; better follow-through
Community Involvement	Uplifting collective spirit; improved community bonds
Workplace	Higher morale; reduced turnover; increased job satisfaction

What fascinates me most about this ripple effect is its cumulative nature. The benefits keep building upon each other over time, creating an even bigger impact as the days go by. Positive thinking doesn't just improve individual lives—it creates waves of beneficial effects that reach far beyond ourselves.

PART IV
SHOW WARMTH

14

THE IMPORTANCE OF WARMTH

"Warmth, kindness, and friendship are the most yearned for commodities in the world. The person who can provide them will never be lonely."

~Ann Landers

We all know how amazing it feels to be welcomed with a big smile or a warm hug. In this context, warmth has nothing to do with physical warmth, like being wrapped up in a cozy blanket on a chilly day. For relationships, warmth refers to kindness, genuine interest, and positive regard for others. Think of it as the emotional *"temperature"* we bring into our interactions.

So why is warmth so important in our relationships?

1. **Warmth Helps Build Trust**: Trust is the foundation of any strong relationship, whether it's with family, friends, or co-workers. When we approach people with warmth, it signals that we're trustworthy and have good intentions. This makes others more likely to open up and share their thoughts and feelings with us. Imagine you're meeting someone new; if they greet you with a warm smile and friendly attitude, you're more likely to feel comfortable around them, right? That's because their warmth helps dissolve any initial barriers or skepticism.

2. **Warmth Encourages Cooperation**: We're far more likely to cooperate with someone who treats us kindly and respectfully compared to someone who doesn't. In workplaces, for instance, a manager who shows warmth towards their team can inspire loyalty, higher morale and productivity. People naturally want to work harder for someone who values them as individuals rather than just as employees filling roles. Similarly, at home, showing emotional warmth can encourage unity and harmony among family members.

3. **Warmth Enhances Communication**: Open and effective communication is essential in any relationship. When we approach conversations with warmth, we're more likely to create an environment where others feel safe speaking freely. This doesn't mean we always have to agree with each other, but it does mean listening actively and without judgment. When people feel heard and understood, they're more apt to share openly and honestly.

4. **Warmth Reduces Conflict**: Believe it or not, warmth can be a powerful tool for conflict resolution. By approaching disagreements with kindness and empathy rather than anger or defensiveness, we can often find common ground more quickly. A warm approach shows that we respect the other person's point of view even if we don't necessarily agree with it.

Here's a quick table to illustrate how warmth impacts different aspects of relationships:

ASPECT OF RELATIONSHIP	HOW WARMTH HELPS
Trust	Builds credibility and reliability
Cooperation	Enhances willingness to work together
Communication	Promotes open and honest dialogue
Conflict Resolution	Reduces tension and finds common ground

Think about how you feel when someone really listens to you or shows you appreciation—*doesn't it make your day better?* That's the magic of warmth! And the best part is that displaying warmth doesn't cost anything but has immense benefits for both parties involved.

WARMTH FOR STRONGER CONNECTIONS IN PERSONAL AND WORK SETTINGS

When we talk about connections, both in personal life and at work, I think we can all agree that relationships built on genuine warmth tend to be the strongest. *But why is that? And how can exhibiting warmth transform our relationships for the better?* Let's discuss some practical ways warmth fosters those deep connections we crave.

In personal relationships:

One clear example of warmth making a difference is in how we **interact with family and friends**. Personal relationships come with a lot of warmth. For instance, we are more likely to approach each other with a sincere smile and a hug. This doesn't just make you feel loved; it strengthens your bond with that person. Genuine warmth often translates into acts of kindness and understanding, which go a long way in building trust and intimacy.

For instance, my best friend always knows when I'm having a tough day, even if I haven't said anything. She'll send a quick *"thinking of you"* message or drop by with my favorite coffee. These small gestures, filled with warmth, make me feel seen and valued. Over time, such acts deepen our relationship because they show consistent care and understanding.

In work settings:

Warmth here can significantly impact team cohesion and overall productivity. When team members feel genuinely cared for by their leaders or colleagues, they're more likely to feel comfortable sharing ideas, asking for help, and working collaboratively.

I've worked in companies where the management practices inclusiveness and shows genuine concern for their employees' well-being. For example, one manager always starts meetings by asking how everyone is doing—not as a formality, but because she genuinely cares. This creates a supportive atmosphere where everyone feels valued.

Moreover, demonstrating warmth can aid in conflict resolution at work. When disagreements arise—and they will—a warm approach can diffuse tension quickly. Acknowledging emotions and expressing empathy shows others you're not dismissing their feelings or concerns, which helps find common ground more swiftly.

Here's a simple chart to illustrate how warmth impacts various aspects of work life:

ASPECT	WITHOUT WARMTH	WITH WARMTH
Communication	Limited & guarded	Open & transparent
Collaboration	Resistant & competitive	Cooperative & supportive
Conflict Resolution	Prolonged disputes	Rapid & empathetic resolution
Employee Morale	Low engagement	High satisfaction & motivation

This table shows how integral warmth is to creating productive and pleasant working environments.

In another instance at my workplace, there was an ongoing debate on resource allocation for projects. It had become quite heated until our HR manager intervened with a warm approach. She actively listened to both sides, empathizing with their concerns without taking sides initially. From there, she facilitated constructive dialogue that ultimately led to an agreeable solution for everyone involved.

If we actively choose to incorporate more warmth into our day-to-day interactions—whether at home or work—we'll likely see profound improvements in how deeply connected we feel to those around us.

Reinforcing Team Spirit Through Warm Gestures

In one of my previous jobs, we had a tradition where we celebrated each team member's birthday with a small gathering, birthday cake, and a card with personal notes of appreciation. I remember vividly when it was my turn; the team leader gave a heartfelt speech about my contributions and handed me a birthday card with notes that everyone signed. Those simple yet warm gestures made me feel incredibly valued. It fostered a deeper sense of belonging and encouraged me to put in extra effort, not because I had to, but because I genuinely wanted to contribute to a team that appreciated me.

This sense of appreciation wasn't just limited to birthdays; we also celebrated professional milestones like project completions and promotions. By recognizing and valuing everyone's efforts through these warm actions, our team became more cohesive and motivated.

Here's how it impacted different areas of our work life:

ASPECT	BEFORE TRADITIONS	AFTER TRADITIONS
Team Spirit	Moderate engagement	High collaboration and support
Work Satisfaction	Average	Significantly increased
Productivity	Steady performance	Marked improvement

CREATING A WARM CUSTOMER EXPERIENCE

I used to manage a retail store/gas station where customer satisfaction was crucial. One day, an older woman came in looking distressed because she had forgotten her purse but needed to purchase some gas urgently. Instead of turning her away, I assured her that she could fill-up her car now and come back later to pay. Her eyes welled up with gratitude as she thanked me profusely.

A week later, she returned not just to pay for her gas but also brought homemade cookies for everyone as a thank-you gesture. This simple act of warmth went beyond mere customer service; it created a loyal bond between us and the customer who felt genuinely cared for.

In another instance, during the holiday season, we gave gifts to our customers. These warm initiatives didn't just improve customer relationships—they also boosted employee morale and drew more people into our store. By embracing warmth in our interactions, both personal and professional relationships flourished into meaningful and lasting connections.

Here's how these efforts translated into tangible benefits:

METRIC	BEFORE INITIATIVES	AFTER INITIATIVES
Customer Retention	Moderate	High
Community Engagement	Limited	Strong presence
Employee Morale	Satisfactory	Elevated enthusiasm

WORKSHEET
Measuring Your Warmth Towards Others

It's important to self-reflect on how we interact with those around us. This simple worksheet can help you gauge your level of warmth in personal and work settings. And as always, answer honestly to get the most accurate reflection.

1. Personal Interactions:

How often do you greet your family and friends with a smile or hug?

- Frequently
- Sometimes
- Rarely

Do you check in with your loved ones when they seem down?

- Always
- Occasionally
- Never

How often do you perform small acts of kindness (e.g., making coffee, sending a thoughtful message)?

- Almost daily
- Weekly
- Seldom

2. Workplace Interactions:

Do you ask your colleagues how they are genuinely doing during meetings?

- Regularly
- Occasionally
- Not at all

How do you handle disagreements with colleagues? (Choose the closest response)

- With empathy and active listening
- By staying neutral and factual
- With frustration or avoidance

Do you encourage collaboration and support within your team?

- Actively promote it
- Sometimes support it
- Rarely make an effort

PERSONAL SCORE			
INTERACTION	FREQUENTLY	SOMETIMES	RARELY
Greeting with a smile or hug			
Checking in when they're down			
Small acts of kindness			

WORKPLACE SCORE			
INTERACTION	FREQUENTLY	SOMETIMES	RARELY
Asking genuinely during meetings			
Handling disagreements empathetically			
Encouraging teamwork			

Take a moment to review your answers. Are there areas you'd like to improve on? Reflect on what changes you can make to show more warmth in both your personal life and at work.

Remember, even small gestures can lead to deeper, more meaningful connections.

15

DEVELOPING WARMTH

―――•••••―――

"Keep a cool head and a warm heart."

~Mike Love

As we've established, warmth fosters trust and compassion in our relationships, both personal and professional. When we project warmth, people are naturally drawn to us. They feel safe, valued, and understood, hence our relationships become more meaningful.

A warm attitude can change the atmosphere of an entire room—it's contagious. When we show warmth, it encourages others to do the same, creating a positive ripple effect that can touch everyone we encounter. In challenging times, warmth becomes even more essential as it provides comfort and reassurance to those who need it most.

CULTIVATING EMPATHY

Empathy is the cornerstone of warmth. It's about putting ourselves in someone else's shoes and understanding their feelings and perspectives. Empathy goes beyond just feeling sorry for someone; it's about truly understanding and sharing the feelings of another.

Cultivating empathy begins with being present and attentive to those around us. Take time to listen without interrupting, offering your full attention. Besides showing that you care, this helps you truly understand where the other person is coming from.

Let's break down some practical steps for cultivating empathy, which in turn helps us develop warmth in our personal and professional relationships.

1. Challenge Yourself: If we stay within our comfort zone, it's hard to grow in any area, including empathy. This means you need to deliberately push yourself out of your comfort zone. For me, this involves engaging in activities or situations that I'm not naturally drawn to. It could be something as simple as striking up a conversation with a stranger or volunteering for a cause I know little about.

The key here is to break through your personal barriers and explore new terrain. I remember when I first joined a local community center to help teach English to immigrants. It was quite intimidating, but the experience opened my eyes to many different perspectives and lives, which greatly boosted my empathy. Aim to expose yourself to people with different backgrounds so that you can broaden your perspectives.

2. Get Out of Your Usual Environment: Sometimes, our usual surroundings can create a bubble that hinders our ability to see beyond our everyday experiences. Getting out of your usual environment can be incredibly enlightening. Travel if you can, or even just explore parts of your town or city that you don't typically visit. By doing so, you expose yourself to different ways of life or different struggles people face.

Once, I joined a neighborhood clean-up initiative in a part of town I rarely visited. The people I met and the stories I heard made me realize how disconnected I'd been from these community issues.

3. Get Feedback: Feedback is essential for personal growth and understanding how others perceive you. Sometimes we think we're coming across one way when, in reality, others are getting a very different message.

Ask trusted friends or colleagues for honest feedback about your interactions and how empathetic you appear to them. Don't just seek approval; ask them for areas where you could improve and make a conscious effort to act on their suggestions.

4. Explore the Heart, Not Just the Head: Empathy isn't just an intellectual exercise; it requires emotional involvement too. When listening to someone else's story, try to feel their emotions as well as understand their words. This means paying attention not only to what they are saying but also to how they are feeling—reading between the lines, so to speak.

For instance, when a friend shared her struggles with me about dealing with a difficult family situation, I made an effort not just to listen but also to emotionally connect with her pain and challenges. To do this, you need to try to really feel what the other person is going through. Ask yourself, *if you were going through the same thing, how would it make you feel?*

5. Walk in Others' Shoes: This phrase might sound cliché, but its practice still stands. To cultivate true empathy, you need to actually walk in other people's shoes—both metaphorically and sometimes literally! Try living a day in someone else's circumstances if possible.

Volunteer at shelters or participate in programs that allow you access to lives vastly different from your own.

It's easy to judge from the outside; it's much harder but more rewarding to understand from within.

6. Examine Your Biases: We all have biases; it's normal. However, recognizing these biases is crucial for developing genuine empathy. Take some time for self-reflection and identify any prejudices or preconceived notions you may hold about people different from yourself, whether those differences are cultural, economic, racial, or otherwise. Acknowledging these biases is the first step towards overcoming them.

You can use the table below to brainstorm:

My Biases and Prejudices		
Category	Bias	Truth
Cultural		
Racial		
Economic		
General		

7. Cultivate Your Sense of Curiosity: Curiosity drives understanding and connection like nothing else can. Cultivating this curiosity means actively seeking out stories and perspectives different from our own. Read diverse books, watch documentaries about various cultures or issues you're unfamiliar with, engage in difficult conversations instead of shying away from them—all with an open heart and mind. As you do, ask open-ended questions like *"How did that make you feel?"* or *"What was that experience like for you?"* Keep digging deeper until you've truly understood a perspective different from your own.

8. Ask Better Questions: Lastly, asking better questions can make all the difference in meaningful communication and empathy development. Instead of superficial questions like *"How are you?"*, try more open-ended ones that invite deeper conversation. These can be questions like *"What has been challenging for you recently?"* or *"Can you tell me more about your experiences growing up?"* These kinds of questions open the door for people to share more deeply, allowing you to better understand their feelings and experiences.

Remember that every little step counts towards creating deeper connections and understanding in our increasingly divided world. The journey may be tricky and uncomfortable at times, but the rewards will be immeasurable, for both yourself and those around you.

ACTIVE LISTENING SKILLS

Have you ever been in a conversation where you felt genuinely heard and understood? There's something incredibly affirming about it. That's the magic of active listening, and it's a skill that not only fosters better communication but also helps in developing warmth in our relationships.

Active listening means that you hear the words, but also you are entirely present with the other person, both mentally and emotionally.

Now, let's see how we can develop these skills:

1. Pay Attention and Be Present:

This might seem obvious, but in today's world of constant distractions, genuinely paying attention takes effort. Put away your phone, avoid thinking about what you'll say next, and focus entirely on the person in front of you.

Being completely present isn't as easy as it sounds. Our minds wander, especially during longer conversations or when we're tired or stressed. Here are a few tips that might help:

    a. *Mindfulness:* Practice mindfulness techniques like focusing on your breath for a few minutes before engaging in serious conversations.

    b. *Environment:* Choose an environment conducive to conversation—somewhere quiet without too many distractions.

    c. *Set Intentions:* Before starting a conversation, set an intention to be fully present and listen actively.

2. Feedback Techniques:

Reflect back on what the person is saying by paraphrasing or summarizing their points. You might say something like, *"What I'm hearing is…"* or *"It sounds like you're saying…"*. This not only shows that you've been listening but also clarifies any misunderstandings. Just be sure not to interrupt them to seek feedback—wait for a pause.

When it comes to paraphrasing and summarizing, here is how they can be used effectively:

a. *Paraphrasing:* If someone says, "I've been feeling really overwhelmed at work lately," you might paraphrase with, "It sounds like your job has been quite stressful recently."

b. *Summarizing:* After a lengthy explanation from someone about their situation, summarize by saying something like, *"So basically, you're dealing with A, B, and C at the same time."*

Both techniques confirm that you've understood what was shared and allow the speaker to correct anything if needed.

3. Avoiding Judgment:

Hold off on forming opinions or jumping to conclusions while the other person is speaking. Everyone has a story to tell, and everyone deserves the chance to be heard without judgment.

True, we all have our biases and preconceived notions, but when we are truly listening, it's crucial to keep these in check. By suspending judgment, we create a safer space for the speaker to share openly.

a. *Practice Curiosity:* Instead of judging, get curious. Ask open-ended questions like, "Can you tell me more about that?" or "What led you to feel this way?"

b. *Acknowledge Differences:* Recognize that everyone has different experiences and perspectives. It's okay to not always agree; what's important is to listen without immediate criticism.

c. *Be Patient:* Give the speaker the time they need to express themselves without rushing them or interrupting.

4. Respond Appropriately:

Finally, after they've finished speaking, respond thoughtfully. Whether it's offering advice (if asked for) or just empathizing with their feelings, make sure your response is supportive.

WORKSHEET
Active Listening Skills

Now that we've discussed the essentials of active listening skills, let's put them into practice with a simple worksheet:

1. How can I remind myself to keep an open mind during conversations?

_____

_____

_____

_____

2. What are some ways I can practice empathy in my daily interactions?

_____

_____

_____

_____

3. List two biases you have recognized in yourself and how you plan to address them:

Bias 1:

_____

_____

Plan:

_____

_____

_____

_____

_____

Bias 2:

_____

_____

Plan:

_____

_____

_____

_____

4. Write down a clarifying question you can ask if you're unsure about something someone has said:

_____
_____
_____
_____

5. How can I show verbal acknowledgment when someone is sharing their feelings with me?

_____
_____
_____
_____

6. Why is it important to avoid offering solutions immediately during conversations?

_____
_____
_____
_____

Remember, becoming a better listener takes practice. Be patient with yourself as you develop these skills, and understand that every conversation presents an opportunity to improve your active listening abilities.

NON-VERBAL COMMUNICATION

Non-verbal communication forms a massive part of how we communicate warmth and understanding. This is all about those subtle, yet powerful, ways we express ourselves without using words. It's the language of our bodies, eyes, and even our touch. Sometimes, what we don't say can communicate more than the words that come out of our mouths.

I think of non-verbal cues as the music in a movie—it sets the tone and can often tell you more about what's happening than the actual dialogue.

1. Body Language

This can be as simple as nodding your head to show you're listening or as complex as using your entire body to express enthusiasm or concern. Open body language tends to make people feel at ease.

Did you know that a warm smile can make you seem more approachable and friendly? It's true! Smiling not only makes you feel good but also transmits positive vibes to those around you. So, the next time you meet someone new or greet an old friend, give them a genuine smile.

Another key aspect of body language is eye contact. Maintaining good eye contact shows that you're engaged and interested in the conversation. However, don't overdo it as staring can make people feel uncomfortable. A good rule of thumb is to hold eye contact for about 3-5 seconds at a time before briefly looking away. This balance helps you connect with others without making them feel uneasy.

2. Posture

Standing straight with your shoulders back exudes confidence and openness. When you're talking to someone, face them directly and lean in slightly.

This shows that you are fully present and interested in what they have to say. Avoid crossing your arms, as this can come across as defensive or closed-off.

Using **open gestures**, like keeping your palms up or out while speaking, signals that you are open and inviting discussion. Try to avoid fidgeting or touching your face too much; these actions can distract from your message and might make you appear anxious.

3. Touch

We can't forget about the power of touch in non-verbal communication. A gentle pat on the back, a warm handshake, or even a light touch on the arm can create a feeling of connection and trust. Of course, it's essential to be mindful of personal boundaries and cultural differences when it comes to touch.

Keep in mind that space also influences our interactions—something called **proxemics**. The amount of personal space someone needs can vary depending on their culture and personality. Standing too close might make someone feel uncomfortable, while standing too far might make you seem distant or disinterested. A good practice is to be observant of how the other person reacts and adjust accordingly.

4. Tone

One thing we can't ignore is the tone of our voice. A warm tone can make even simple words come alive with kindness and empathy. Try speaking in a soft yet clear voice with enough inflection to show enthusiasm without overwhelming the listener.

To help visualize these tips, here's a simple table summarizing key non-verbal cues:

NON-VERBAL CUE	HOW IT DEVELOPS WARMTH
Smile	Conveys friendliness and approachability
Eye Contact	Shows engagement and interest
Posture	Displays confidence and openness
Gestures	Signals openness (e.g., open palms)
Touch	Creates connection (e.g., handshake)
Personal Space	Respects comfort levels; adjusts per individual
Tone of Voice	Adds warmth through gentle inflections

Remember that consistency is vital when practicing these non-verbal cues. Additionally, being authentic in your expressions will naturally make others feel comfortable around you.

16

WARMTH IN EVERYDAY INTERACTIONS

"Let us not forget the moments of tenderness in one moment of hatred. Let us not forget the light of warmth in one moment of iciness. Let us not forget the moments of endearment in one moment of aloofness."

~Jayita Bhattacharjee

Learning is one thing, and applying what we learn is another. We've seen the benefits of showing warmth and touched on one essential aspect that facilitates warmth—empathy. In this chapter, we will see how to naturally exemplify warmth in everyday interactions so that we can turn it into an instinct.

Before this happens, you will need to actively look for opportunities to show warmth. Keep in mind that whenever you encounter someone, whether a random stranger or someone you personally know, there's always an opportunity.

SMALL ACTS OF KINDNESS

Small acts of kindness can be as simple as smiling at a stranger or as involved as helping a neighbor in need. No matter how small, these gestures can transform not just another person's day but also our own.

1. Use Your Words

One of the easiest ways to show warmth is through our words. A sincere compliment can go a long way. Whether it's acknowledging someone's hard work or simply admiring their outfit, kind words have an incredible power to uplift spirits.

I remember once when I complimented a colleague on her presentation skills after a stressful meeting. Her face lit up immediately, and she later told me that my words boosted her confidence and lit up her day.

2. Small Acts

Small acts of kindness don't always require words. Sometimes, actions speak louder. Holding the door for someone, letting a driver merge into your lane, or even picking up trash from the sidewalk are all simple gestures that show care for others and our community.

Even online, there are countless opportunities for showing warmth. A thoughtful email or a supportive comment on social media can have the same positive impact as face-to-face interactions. Whenever I see someone sharing an achievement or struggle online, I make it a point to leave an encouraging comment or send a message of support.

Food is a universal language and another beautiful way to share warmth and kindness. Baking cookies for your neighbor, sharing lunch with a coworker who forgot theirs at home, or cooking dinner for a sick friend are all acts that nourish both body and soul.

Acts of service also speak volumes about warmheartedness. Simple but strong gestures like helping someone carry bags, offering your seat on public transport, or volunteering your time for community service make a tangible difference in people's lives. One time, while traveling by bus during rush hour, I offered my seat to an older woman who looked tired. She was grateful, and we ended up discussing her many travel adventures throughout her life. It truly was an enriching conversation for both of us.

Random acts of kindness create ripples that spread far beyond the initial act. When someone experiences warmth and generosity from you, they're more likely to pass it on to others. In this way, everyone becomes part of a larger cycle of positivity and compassion.

But these small acts don't only benefit others; they bring joy and fulfillment into our own lives too. Knowing we've made a positive impact gives us a sense of purpose and connection with the world around us.

To make it easier for you to incorporate more warmth into your daily routine, here's a quick reference chart with simple actions you can take:

SMALL ACT	HOW IT HELPS OTHERS	HOW IT BENEFITS YOU
Smile at Someone	Brightens their day	Elevates mood
Give Compliments	Boosts confidence	Creates stronger connections
Genuinely Listen	Makes people feel valued	Enhances relationships
Offer Help	Provides needed support	Fosters empathy
Send Thoughtful Messages	Shows care	Strengthens bonds
Share Food	Offers comfort	Brings joy through giving
Engage in Service	Contributes to community well-being	Cultivates purpose

When we become aware of these moments and seize them with intention, our lives become richer and more fulfilling. We can turn ordinary interactions into meaningful experiences that leave a lasting impression.

THE IMPACT OF GIVING BACK

Every morning, I try to remind myself that the smallest acts of kindness can make a big difference. I'm not talking about grand gestures, but the simple, everyday interactions that can transform someone's day. Over time, I've realized how essential it is to incorporate warmth into my daily routine and the powerful effect it has, not just on others but on myself too.

I remember one of my neighbors from a few years ago, Mrs. Garcia. She was an older lady who lived alone and often struggled with her groceries. One chilly morning, as I was heading out for a jog, I saw her trying to carry bags that seemed far too heavy for her frail frame. My instinct was to stop and help. The smile she gave me after that small act of help warmed my heart more than words can describe. From then on, whenever I saw her, even if just a simple "Good morning," the connection we had brightened both our days.

In our hustle and bustle life, it's easy to overlook these simple interactions. Yet studies have shown that these moments of warmth significantly impact our mental well-being. Take, for example, the research conducted by sociologist Nicholas Christakis at Yale University, which emphasizes how spreading kindness through social networks can have a ripple effect. When one person engages in an act of kindness, it inspires others within their network to do the same.

One way I've made it a habit to give back is through volunteering. Whether it's at the local soup kitchen or mentoring younger colleagues at work, these activities have reinforced my understanding of warmth in interactions. Another incredible thing about giving back is that it expands our capacity for empathy. Consider this: each time we extend warmth and generosity to others, we're subtly teaching ourselves how to be more empathetic individuals.

For instance, during last winter's cold snap in my city, I decided to hand out hot cocoa and blankets around areas where homeless people often gathered. The conversations I had during those moments deepened my appreciation for their experiences and struggles.

Sometimes, giving back doesn't necessarily need direct face-to-face contact; it can be through initiatives like donations or community support programs. For years now, I've been involved with an initiative where we collect books and school supplies for children in underprivileged areas. Those kids may never know who I am personally, but knowing they're benefiting from something I've contributed warms me in ways that remind me why it's crucial never to stop giving back.

But remember that beyond volunteering or giving back formally, it's about showing warmth by layering kindness into our day-to-day lives through the people we encounter.

ACTIONS	IMPACT ON INDIVIDUALS
Helping older people (like Mrs. Garcia)	Increased community bonding
Spontaneous compliments	Enhanced mood and self-esteem
Volunteering (soup kitchens/mentoring)	Lowered stress levels; increased sense of purpose
Providing empathy through service	Improved social connections; expanded empathy spectrum
Donations/community support programs	Wider reach impact beyond personal circles

From my personal experience and these observations over years of engaging with people from diverse backgrounds—both voluntarily and inadvertently—I can firmly say kindness fosters more solid human bonds than we may initially expect.

However small your actions might seem, they don't go unnoticed. Think about all the positive changes you could bring into someone else's life simply by pausing momentarily from your schedule to show some warmth!

If there's one takeaway here, it would be to challenge yourself bit by bit towards nurturing an instinctive compassion culture that gradually becomes who you are, not just something you practice.

CREATING A WELCOMING ENVIRONMENT

A welcoming environment sets the tone for offering warmth and makes the other person more open and receptive. When people feel comfortable and safe, they are more at ease, and it becomes easier to connect authentically.

Before diving into the physical aspects, here are two simple ways you can use to put people at ease:

Call them by name:

One thing we shouldn't overlook is the power of names. Addressing someone by their name immediately makes the interaction more personal and warmer.

It can sometimes catch people off guard because it's become rare these days, but it usually leaves them smiling. Of course, this works if you know the other person by name. If not, you can ask them their name (if you are in a position to).

Another important point worth noting is being genuinely curious about the lives of others. Asking open-ended questions about their day, their interests, or their families can show that you care. It not only makes the other person feel valued but also enriches your own perspective.

Use Humor:

Humor also plays an essential role in creating warmth in interactions, but remember that it must be used aptly depending on the context (see our section on humor for tips on this)! Light-hearted jokes or funny anecdotes can relieve tension and make people feel more comfortable around you.

Now, our environment plays such an important part in our emotional well-being. Let's see how we can make spaces inviting too—both shared spaces like offices or communal areas at home (for shared offices, make sure you have the authority to make such changes first or consult the respective parties):

ASPECT	TIP
Lighting	Use soft lighting; avoid harsh fluorescents
Decor	Add personal touches like photos or artwork
Seating Arrangement	Create cozy nooks; use comfortable furniture
Cleanliness	Keep areas tidy; declutter regularly
Smell	Use pleasant scents like lavender or vanilla
Temperature	Ensure comfortable room temperature

I once visited a friend who had lit some candles around her living room right before I arrived. The subtle lavender scent combined with dim lighting made me feel instantly welcome and set a relaxed tone for our conversation.

Being timely also contributes to a welcoming environment. Punctuality is a sign of respect and shows that you value the other person's time. If you're always running late or canceling plans last minute, it can make interactions feel rushed and unimportant.

Remember that when it comes to creating warmth, it's often the little things that count. It's those smiles, eye contact, listening ears, and clean, inviting spaces that build a welcoming environment conducive to positivity and connection.

17

OVERCOMING BARRIERS TO WARMTH

"True beauty is a warm heart, a kind soul, and an attentive ear."

~Ken Poirot

The truth is, being warm and open isn't always easy. We often face several barriers that can prevent us from expressing our true selves and connecting with others. It's important to recognize these barriers and actively work to overcome them.

Why? Overcoming these challenges allows us to form deeper connections, both in our personal lives and in our professional endeavors. There is so much value in being approachable and relatable — it not only enriches your interactions but also helps you grow personally.

When it comes to barriers to being open, two culprits often hold us back: **unresolved shyness** and **social anxiety.** These two can significantly limit your opportunities for meaningful interactions. Suppose you constantly find yourself held back by an inability to engage with others. In that case, you know how it feels to miss out on forming genuine relationships that could support your emotional well-being or professional growth.

Moreover, breaking down emotional walls is essential for mental health. When you put up barriers, you're essentially isolating yourself emotionally. This isolation can lead to feelings of loneliness and may even contribute to depression over time.

So, it's clear that if we want to show up fully for life, we need to tackle these barriers head-on.

DEALING WITH SHYNESS

Shyness is the feeling of discomfort or inhibition in social situations—it's that fluttery feeling in your stomach or the anxiety that makes your palms all sweaty. At some point, we've all been there! The good news is that shyness isn't a fixed trait; it's something you can work on and improve over time.

Understanding where your shyness comes from is an essential first step. For many people, shyness starts in childhood and can be influenced by various factors such as genetics, upbringing, and past experiences. For instance, if you were raised in a very reserved household where social interactions were limited, you might find it more challenging to open up as an adult. Also, negative experiences such as bullying can play a role in making someone more shy (you will be able to identify your triggers in the upcoming worksheet).

Once you've identified the root causes of your shyness, you can start working on strategies to overcome it:

1. Preparation is Key: If you know you're going into a situation that makes you feel shy or anxious, preparation can be your best friend.

For example, if you're going to a party where you don't know many people, think of some topics or questions you might want to ask new acquaintances. Consider the kind of party you are going to and the kind of "scene" it will be. This can give you pointers on the type of questions to ask.

Preparation takes the pressure off having to come up with something on the spot.

2. Gradual Exposure: Start small and gradually increase your exposure to social situations. If large groups make you uncomfortable, start by interacting with one person at a time and build from there.

This gradual approach will build up your confidence and make larger social settings less intimidating over time.

3. Positive Visualization: Remember our section on visualization? You can use the power of visualization here too! Picture yourself successfully navigating through social scenarios before you actually experience them.

Visualize yourself walking into a room confidently, engaging in conversations smoothly, and leaving the event feeling good about yourself. This mental rehearsal can do wonders for reducing anxiety.

4. Seek Supportive Environments: Surround yourself with people who are encouraging and supportive. Being in a nurturing environment can significantly reduce your anxiety and make social interactions more comfortable.

Find and join clubs, groups, or communities where the focus is on mutual interests rather than social ability.

5. Practice Self-Compassion: Be kind to yourself when things don't go perfectly. Everyone has awkward moments, and it's important not to dwell on them. Recognize that overcoming shyness is a journey that will have ups and downs.

6. Body Language: Sometimes the way you carry yourself can influence how you feel inside. Practice confident body language — stand tall, make eye contact, and smile. These actions can trick your brain into feeling more confident.

7. Professional Help: If shyness is severely impacting your life, it might be worth seeking help from a therapist or counselor. They can offer tailored advice and coping strategies.

WORKSHEET
Personal Shyness Breakdown And Strategy Plan

1. Identify Triggers: When do you feel the most shy (e.g., meeting new people, public speaking)?

_____

_____

_____

_____

_____

2. Recognize Root Causes: Reflect on your past experiences or upbringing that might contribute to your shyness.

_____

_____

_____

_____

_____

3. Preparation Techniques: What can you prepare or think of beforehand to ease your anxiety?

_____
_____
_____
_____
_____

4. Gradual Exposure Goals: List small social goals that you can start with (e.g., saying hi to a coworker).

_____
_____
_____
_____
_____

5. Positive Visualization Scenarios: Describe a social scenario you're anxious about and how you would like it to go.

_____
_____
_____
_____
_____

6. Supportive Social Circles: Identify supportive friends or groups you can spend time with.

_____
_____
_____
_____
_____
_____

7. Self-Compassion Reminders: Write down ways to be kind to yourself after a challenging social interaction.

_____
_____
_____
_____
_____
_____

By filling out this worksheet honestly and actively working on these steps, you'll start seeing improvements over time. Keep at it! And as you work your way towards overcoming shyness, remember to celebrate the small victories along the way.

Alonzo Johnson, Ph.D.

MANAGING SOCIAL ANXIETY

When we talk about warmth in social settings, social anxiety is an obvious and major barrier. I have been there too. Your palms start sweating, your heart races, and you feel like taking to your heels! But overcoming this anxiety is not just crucial for developing connections but also for showing up fully in our lives.

Just like shyness, one of the first steps toward managing social anxiety is understanding what triggers it. Many people experience anxiety in social situations because they fear judgment or rejection. For me, it was always the thought that I would say something stupid or make a fool of myself. However, knowing your triggers and acknowledging them is a big part of overcoming them.

Let's address how to handle these feelings head-on:

1. Gradual Exposure

I know this might sound terrifying, but gradual exposure is essentially about facing your fears, bit by bit, in controlled ways. Start small—maybe it's joining a casual conversation at work or attending a gathering where you're somewhat comfortable.

The more you expose yourself to these situations, the more you realize that your worst fears often don't come true.

2. Breathe and Take A Step Back

While exposure is vital, having practical tools to handle anxiety in the moment can make a world of difference. Deep breathing exercises have worked wonders for me.

When you slow down your breathing, you send signals to your brain that it's time to relax. Inhale deeply for four seconds, hold the breath for four seconds, and then exhale for another four seconds. Repeat this until you start feeling calmer.

Additionally, sometimes finding distractions during stressful moments can help manage the intensity of those feelings. I've found that focusing on something trivial—like counting tiles on the floor or reciting lyrics from favorite songs—can divert my mind long enough for the wave of anxiety to pass.

3. Cognitive Restructuring

This involves rethinking how you interpret social situations. Our minds can be our worst enemies—we often jump to the worst-case scenario automatically.

The next time you catch yourself thinking, *"Everyone thinks I'm stupid,"* challenge that thought: *"Is there any real evidence that supports this?"* Often, you'll find there's none.

4. Prepare

Preparation and practice also apply when it comes to dealing with social anxiety. If a specific type of social interaction triggers your anxiety—like public speaking—you can prepare for it extensively until you feel more confident about handling it.

Rehearse what you're going to say, do a mock presentation in front of close friends or even in front of a mirror. This can build up your confidence gradually.

5. Social Skills Training Programs

These can also be beneficial if you struggle with making connections. These programs often offer structured environments where you can practice social interactions with guidance and feedback.

6. Seek Help

If you find that your social anxiety severely impacts your daily life despite trying various strategies on your own, seeking help from a therapist can provide additional support and techniques tailored specifically to you.

Peer support groups are another excellent resource where you can meet others who are facing similar challenges. Sharing experiences and strategies can provide both relief and new ideas on managing anxiety.

In short, overcoming barriers to warmth through managing social anxiety involves a combination of self-awareness, practical tools like deep breathing and cognitive restructuring, preparation and practice, seeking professional help when necessary, and finding community support.

BREAKING DOWN EMOTIONAL WALLS

We all carry emotional walls within us, built from past experiences, fear of vulnerability, or simply not knowing how to connect with others. Those walls can isolate us and prevent us from forming meaningful relationships.

Let's acknowledge that these walls didn't appear overnight. They were constructed over time, often as protective mechanisms.

Recognizing the root cause of our emotional barriers is the stepping stone to dismantling them.

One effective way to identify these causes is through self-reflection. Take some quiet time alone and ask yourself questions like, *"When did I start feeling disconnected?"* or *"What experiences made me wary of opening up?"*

Journaling your thoughts can also help in pinpointing specific events or influences that contributed to the building of your walls. Here's a simple exercise you can follow:

1. When did I start feeling disconnected?

_____

_____

_____

_____

_____

_____

2. What specific events contributed to this?

_____

_____

_____

_____

_____

_____

3. How do I feel when I try to open up emotionally?

_____

_____

_____

_____

_____

4. What fears arise when I consider being vulnerable?

_____

_____

_____

_____

_____

5. How has this affected my relationships so far?

_____

_____

_____

_____

_____

Once you have insights from your self-reflection, it becomes easier to take actionable steps:

Step 1: Practice Self-Compassion

Be kind to yourself. Understand that everyone carries scars, and it's okay to have emotional walls. Don't judge yourself for having them; instead, show yourself the same kindness and understanding you would offer a friend in need.

Step 2: Communicate Openly

Start small by sharing minor thoughts or feelings with someone you trust. Over time, increase the depth of your sharing. Communication is a muscle that gets stronger with use.

For instance, instead of just saying *"I'm fine"* after a stressful day at work, try something like, *"It was a hectic day at work; I felt overwhelmed by the amount of tasks."*

Step 3: Build Trust Gradually

Trust isn't built in a day, so take it slow and easy on yourself. Spend time with people who make you feel comfortable and understood. Share experiences together—whether it's through attending events, cooking a meal together, or simply having regular conversations.

Step 4: Embrace Vulnerability

Being emotionally open makes us feel vulnerable, and that's okay. It's this very vulnerability that allows authentic connections to flourish.

Instead of avoiding situations where you might feel exposed emotionally, face them head-on with courage.

Step 5: Create a Support System

Having a support system is crucial. Surround yourself with people who understand you and encourage your growth. This could be friends, family, or even support groups where members share similar experiences. Building this network can provide a sense of security as you work on dismantling your walls.

Step 6: Celebrate Small Wins

Acknowledge and celebrate progress, no matter how minor it may seem. Each step towards emotional openness is a win, whether it's sharing your feelings more openly or experiencing deeper connections. By celebrating these milestones, you reinforce positive behavior and motivate yourself to continue pushing forward.

Step 7: Engage in Mindfulness Practices

Mindfulness practices such as meditation, yoga, or breathing exercises can help you stay grounded and in touch with your emotions. These practices teach you to observe your feelings without judgment, allowing you to process emotions in real time rather than bottling them up.

Step 8: Seek Professional Help

Sometimes we need guidance beyond what self-help strategies can offer. A therapist can provide insights and tools specifically tailored for breaking down emotional barriers.

If you need some help tracking your progress, the table on the next page provides a sample you can adopt for your own progress tracking:

EMOTIONAL GROWTH PROGRESS TRACKER

MILESTONE	DATE ACHIEVED	NOTES/FEELINGS
Identified initial emotional wall	MM/DD/YYYY	Felt relieved to pinpoint the exact cause
Practiced self-compassion	MM/DD/YYYY	Realized the importance of being kind to oneself
Shared minor thoughts with someone trusted	MM/DD/YYYY	Felt nervous but also lighter after sharing
Embraced vulnerability in conversation	MM/DD/YYYY	Experienced deeper connection with a friend
Sought professional help	MM/DD/YYYY	Gained new insights

Overcoming emotional barriers is a path filled with ups and downs, but each effort you make brings you closer to forming those meaningful, heartfelt connections. Remember that this journey is ongoing and won't happen all at once. And when you experience setbacks, don't forget that they are part of the process—not failures.

PART V
BE UNSELFISH

18

UNDERSTANDING UNSELFISHNESS

"Unselfishness is contagious."

~Larry Nance, Jr.

Life, for most of us, is a long and winding journey filled with countless decisions, challenges, and opportunities. *One question that often arises is: What does it mean to live a fulfilling and meaningful life?* From my experience and understanding, one fundamental aspect stands out—selflessness or unselfishness.

When we talk about selflessness, we're referring to the act of placing the needs and happiness of others above our own. This doesn't mean neglecting ourselves or becoming martyrs. Instead, it's about finding a balance where we can uplift others while still maintaining our well-being.

Being unselfish is more than just a noble idea; it's a mindset that shapes how we interact with the world around us. It's embedded in simple acts such as listening to someone without interrupting, lending a helping hand without expecting anything in return, or making sacrifices for the greater good. Essentially, it's about contributing to something bigger than ourselves.

Why is unselfishness essential?

1. Being Unselfish Helps Cultivate Empathy

As we pay attention to the needs and feelings of others, we become more attuned to their experiences. This fosters deeper connections and makes us better friends, partners, parents, or colleagues.

Think about a time when someone went out of their way to help you without expecting anything in return. *How did that make you feel?* By doing the same for others, you spread positivity and kindness.

2. Fosters Teamwork

In any group situation—be it at work, school, or within a community project—success often hinges on the ability of individuals to work together harmoniously.

When you're unselfish, you're willing to listen to different viewpoints and collaborate more effectively. This collective approach leads to better solutions and fosters an environment where everyone feels valued and respected.

3. Personal Satisfaction

Acts of kindness and generosity trigger the release of endorphins in our brains—those are your body's natural feel-good chemicals. So, when you help someone out or share your resources for the greater good, you experience a sense of joy and fulfillment that material possessions just can't match.

4. Health and Wellbeing

Did you know that being unselfish can also improve your mental health? Studies show that people who regularly engage in altruistic activities tend to have lower levels of stress and anxiety.

They exhibit higher levels of emotional well-being because positive social behaviors reinforce our sense of purpose in life.

5. Spreading the Kindness

We often underestimate the ripple effect our actions can have on others. A single act of kindness can inspire both the recipient and observers to pay it forward in countless ways.

This can be backed by the philosophy of *"paying it forward."* The idea here is that when someone does a good deed for you, instead of paying them back directly, you pass on a good deed to another person. This creates an ongoing chain reaction of generosity that benefits not just individuals but whole communities.

Incorporating selfless behavior into our daily lives not only enriches our personal experiences but also has a ripple effect on the broader community. It creates an environment where empathy and cooperation thrive—a space where everyone has the opportunity to flourish.

EXAMPLES OF UNSELFISH BEHAVIOR IMPACTING SUCCESS

I always find it remarkable how small acts of unselfishness can snowball into significant impact, both for individuals and communities.

Let me share some examples that I find truly inspiring:

Fred Rogers

One story that continues to resonate with me is about Fred Rogers, the beloved television host from *"Mister Rogers' Neighborhood."* In an industry often driven by ratings and profits, Fred Rogers was unyieldingly focused on the emotional and social development of children.

He was known for his thoughtful and gentle approach to complex issues like divorce and death, always putting children's understanding and well-being at the forefront. His unselfish dedication didn't just create successful TV programming; it fostered a generation of more empathetic and emotionally intelligent individuals.

Warren Buffett

Many people know Warren Buffett as one of the wealthiest individuals on earth, but his commitment to philanthropy is equally noteworthy. Buffett has pledged to give away 99% of his wealth to charitable causes through the Gates Foundation.

This act may seem like an enormous sacrifice, but in reality, it has greatly amplified his influence and legacy far beyond financial success alone. His charitable giving inspires numerous others who have funds to spare to consider how they can also leave a lasting positive impact.

Corrie Ten Boom

Corrie was another person whose unselfish actions had a significant impact during difficult times. Living during World War II in Nazi-occupied Netherlands, Corrie and her family helped hide Jews from persecution—actions that were illegal and highly dangerous at the time.

Their home became known as *"The Hiding Place,"* offering shelter until they were betrayed and arrested. Although she faced immense hardships including imprisonment, Corrie's unselfish efforts saved many lives and her memoir continues to inspire countless others.

Jim Henson

Known for creating The Muppets, Jim Henson had a vision beyond entertainment; he wanted his work to educate children about friendship, empathy, and cultural diversity while making them laugh. He committed himself wholeheartedly to this vision without ego or selfish intent.

Consequently, this led not only to commercial success but also left an indelible mark on generations of children who grew up watching *"Sesame Street"* and *"The Muppet Show."* His ability to combine education with entertainment showcased how putting others first can culminate into lasting success.

Blake Mycoskie

Shifting focus slightly, let's talk about modern-day social entrepreneurship as exemplified by Blake Mycoskie's TOMS Shoes company. When Mycoskie noticed kids in impoverished areas walking without shoes while traveling through Argentina, he established TOMS Shoes under a unique *"one for one"* business model. This meant that for every pair of shoes sold, another pair was given to a child in need.

This mission-centric approach not only helped children but also turned the company into a major commercial success. What started as a simple act of kindness has since evolved; TOMS has expanded its giving model to include eyeglasses, water, safe birth kits, and bullying prevention services.

These stories highlight how acts of unselfish behavior can ripple through communities and history, leading to profound change not just for individuals directly involved but for society at large as well.

WAYS TO PRACTICE UNSELFISHNESS DAILY

Every day is full of opportunities to practice unselfishness, and I've found that the little things we do can make a big difference. Here are some practical ways to incorporate unselfish acts into your daily life:

1. **Listening More, Talking Less:** One of the simplest ways to be unselfish is by genuinely listening to others. When a friend or co-worker is speaking, resist the urge to interrupt and instead give them your full attention. By doing this, you're showing that you value their thoughts and feelings (see more on active listening in Chapter 15).

2. **Sharing Your Time:** Time is such a precious resource, and sharing it with others can be very impactful. Whether it's volunteering at a local shelter, helping a neighbor with groceries, or spending time with family members who need company, dedicating your time to others shows unselfishness in action.

3. **Being There in Small Ways:** Sometimes it's the small gestures that mean the most. Holding the door open for someone, offering your seat on a crowded bus, or letting

someone go ahead of you in line are all acts that demonstrate kindness and consideration.

4. **Sharing Skills and Knowledge:** If you have a particular skill or knowledge area where you excel, offer to help others who might benefit from it. Maybe you can tutor students in a subject you're good at, or help a colleague understand a new software program.

5. **Regular Acts of Kindness:** Incorporate small, unselfish actions into your routine, like sending thank-you notes, complimenting someone's work, or just checking in on friends and family more regularly.

6. **Supporting Others' Success:** Another way of being unselfish is by celebrating other people's successes rather than feeling envious or competitive. You can do this by giving genuine praise when someone accomplishes something great.

7. **Financial Generosity:** Giving financially doesn't have to mean large sums of money; even small donations can make a difference if given unselfishly. Supporting charities or giving tips generously are ways to share your resources with others.

8. **Sharing Meals:** Inviting someone over for dinner or sharing some baked goodies with neighbors not only fosters community but also shows thoughtfulness towards others' well-being.

9. **Patience with Others:** Being patient with those around you can also be an act of unselfishness. Whether it's waiting calmly while someone finishes speaking or being tolerant

when someone makes a mistake, patience shows respect for other people's needs and feelings.

Incorporating these actions into our daily lives doesn't require grand gestures but rather small, consistent efforts that show consideration for others' needs and well-being.

ACTION	EXAMPLE	WHY IT'S UNSELFISH
Listen more	Giving full attention while listening	Shows you value others' feelings
Share time	Volunteering at a local shelter	Contributing valuable personal time
Small helpful acts	Holding doors open	Demonstrates kindness
Sharing skills	Tutoring students	Helps others grow and learn
Acts of kindness	Sending thank-you notes	Makes others feel appreciated
Celebrate successes	Praising colleagues' achievements	Supports positive reinforcement
Financial generosity	Donating to charity	Shares resources
Sharing meals	Inviting neighbors over	Fosters community
Patience	Waiting calmly while someone speaks	Shows respect for their process

WORK SHEET
Self-Assessment on Unselfish Behavior

ACTION	DID I DO THIS TODAY? (YES/NO)	HOW DID IT MAKE ME FEEL?	HOW DID IT IMPACT OTHERS?
Listen more			
Share time			
Small helpful acts			
Sharing skills			
Acts of kindness			
Celebrate successes			
Financial generosity			
Sharing meals			
Patience			

Use this table each day to remind yourself of the different ways you can practice unselfishness. At the end of the day, revisit the actions and reflect on them. Note down whether you accomplished them, how it made you feel, and what effect it had on others.

In addition to daily reflection, consider setting weekly goals for yourself. Identify specific acts of unselfishness you want to focus on and track your progress. This not only helps in creating a consistent habit but also brings awareness to the positive impact you're making.

By committing to these small yet significant acts of unselfishness each day, we can collectively create a more caring and supportive community around us. Let's strive to show up for life with genuine compassion and a willingness to put others before ourselves (however, without losing sight of ourselves in the process).

19

PRACTICING GENEROSITY

"Give what you have. To someone, it may be better than you dare to think."

~Henry Wadsworth Longfellow

It's important to understand this from the start: **true generosity isn't about giving to receive something in return.** It's about offering what you can without any strings attached, and therein lies its real beauty and power. I still remember a moment from my childhood when my dad gave away his favorite old jacket to a stranger on a chilly night. The man was shivering in the cold, and without hesitating, my dad handed over the jacket. He didn't expect anything back—he just saw someone in need and acted. This memory has always stayed with me as a pure example of generosity.

When we practice generosity without expecting anything in return, it changes us internally. It shifts our focus from ourselves to others, effortlessly cultivating empathy and compassion. Studies have shown that acts of generosity can actually boost our mood and even our health!

Here is a simple table that outlines some easy forms of generosity and ideas on how to practice them (we will look at these in depth in just a few):

FORM OF GENEROSITY	IDEAS FOR PRACTICE
Time	Volunteering, Listening to Someone
Knowledge	Teaching a Skill, Sharing Educational Resources
Small Acts of Kindness	Compliments, Opening Doors
Material Gifts	Donating Clothes/Toys, Sharing Food

The challenge that comes with generosity is the expectation factor. It's natural to want acknowledgment for our actions or hope that they will lead to something positive for ourselves down the road. However, true generosity lies in letting go of these desires and just focusing on the act itself.

Interestingly enough, when we give without expecting anything back, we often receive far beyond what we initially offered, not necessarily from the person we helped but from the universe itself in various forms like inner peace and fulfillment.

Here's an example from my own experience: I once helped an elderly neighbor with her yard work every weekend without expecting anything in return. Months later, she introduced me to her granddaughter, who was starting a business and needed help exactly in my line of expertise. That connection turned out to be invaluable for both professional development and personal growth (this is the ripple effect that we discussed earlier).

However difficult it might seem initially, practicing generosity can become second nature over time with conscious effort. Begin with small steps and gradually build up—like any other skill, it develops with practice.

And remember—generosity doesn't always involve grand actions; even the smallest good deed counts significant weight when done out of genuine kindness and goodwill.

VOLUNTEERING YOUR TIME AND RESOURCES

You might think volunteering is just about giving to others, but it's truly a two-way street filled with mutual benefits. It's not only about making an impact on those we help but also about what we gain in return—skills, satisfaction, and a sense of community. For instance, studies show that people who volunteer regularly are happier and feel more fulfilled.

We often overlook how powerful our time can be. When you volunteer, you're more than just a helper; you're a force for positive change. Think about it: your time could mean mentoring a child, cleaning up a local park, or organizing food at a shelter. Each act contributes to building a better world.

Personal Growth and Satisfaction:

When I first started volunteering, I had no idea how profoundly it would affect me. Initially, I did it because I thought it was the right thing to do. But as I got more involved, I realized that the benefits extended far beyond my initial intentions. Volunteering helped me develop new skills like leadership and organization. It also provided me with much-needed perspective on various life situations far different from my own.

Making Connections:

Volunteering is an amazing way to meet new people and expand your social circle. Whether it's working side by side at a food bank or cleaning up local parks, shared experiences bond people. These connections often turn into lifelong friendships or professional networks that can open up new opportunities.

How and Where to Volunteer

Finding the right volunteering opportunity can be as simple as figuring out what you're passionate about.

For instance:

INTEREST/SKILL	AVAILABLE VOLUNTEERING OPPORTUNITIES
Teaching or Mentoring	After-school programs, tutoring centers
Environmental Concerns	Community gardens, cleanup crews
Healthcare	Hospital volunteering, visiting seniors in nursing homes
Animal Welfare	Animal shelters, rescue groups
Event Planning	Fundraisers for local charities

Here are some ways to get started:

1. **Local Nonprofits:** Check out local nonprofits and see if they need any volunteers.

2. **Online Platforms:** Websites like *VolunteerMatch* or *Idealist* can help match you with organizations needing help.

3. **Community Centers:** Many community centers post lists of volunteer opportunities.

4. **Social Media:** Follow the pages of organizations you respect; they often post when they need volunteers.

Remember, volunteering isn't just about giving your time; your resources can also make a massive difference. Donations—whether monetary or material—fill gaps that manpower cannot always cover. Here are simple ways to donate resources:

1. **Money:** Small donations pooled from many individuals can create substantial funding for crucial projects.

2. **Clothes and Supplies:** Items gathering dust at home could be treasures for someone in need.

3. **Skills:** If you have professional skills like graphic design or accounting, many nonprofits could use your expertise for free.

While giving is wonderful, it's important not to overcommit yourself and get burned out. Strike a balance; contribute in ways that fit into your life comfortably so that it remains a fulfilling experience rather than another stressor.

Volunteering your time and resources should feel intrinsically rewarding because it's an active way of showing up for life, not just yours, but for those around you too. Whenever I look back on my experiences with volunteering, I always feel a sense of pride knowing I've left ripples of positive change in various communities.

SUPPORTING CAUSES YOU CARE ABOUT

We all have something we're passionate about. For some, it's animal welfare; for others, it's environmental conservation or advocating for the rights of marginalized communities. Whatever cause resonates with you, supporting it can be profoundly fulfilling. It provides a sense of purpose and allows us to contribute to the greater good.

When I first started getting involved with causes I cared about, I was overwhelmed by the sheer number of ways one could make a difference. But over time, I learned that no contribution is too small. Every bit counts and adds up to significant change over time.

So, how can you support your cause?

1. **Identifying it First:** The first step in supporting a cause is identifying what truly matters to you. Think about what makes you emotional or really inspires you. Is it seeing stray animals? Is it reading stories of children in need? Or maybe it's the headlines about climate change? Everyone has different triggers that drive them to action.

2. **Research and Learn**: Once you've identified your cause, dive deep into understanding it. Read articles, watch documentaries, join online forums, and talk to people already involved. Knowledge is power, and the more informed you are about the issues at hand, the more effectively you can contribute.

3. **Getting Involved Locally**: Sometimes, the most significant impact can be made right in your community. Look for local organizations or chapters of larger organizations that align with your cause. Volunteer your time; many groups thrive

on donations of both time and resources from passionate individuals like you.

4. **Monetary Contributions**: If you're unable to volunteer your time, donating money is another powerful way to support a cause. Many non-profits rely heavily on monetary contributions to fund their activities and initiatives. Even small monthly donations can collectively provide substantial support.

5. **Advocating and Raising Awareness**: Use your voice to raise awareness about your chosen cause. This can be as simple as sharing information on social media, or as involved as organizing events or rallies. Advocacy helps educate others and can drive more people to take action.

6. **Making Lifestyle Changes**: Supporting a cause isn't just about external actions; sometimes it starts at home with lifestyle choices. For instance, if you're passionate about environmental conservation, consider adopting practices such as recycling, reducing plastic use, or using public transportation more frequently—remember, every small act counts.

7. **Collaborating with Others**: Join forces with people who share your passion. Collaboration often leads to innovation and new strategies for addressing issues more effectively.

8. **Measuring Your Impact**: It's important to periodically assess how your contributions are making a difference. This is not necessarily for validation but for understanding areas where more effort might be needed or where strategies might need tweaking.

Below is a simple chart on how you could allocate your support:

WAY TO SUPPORT	TIME COMMITMENT	FINANCIAL COMMITMENT	EXAMPLE ACTIONS
Volunteering	High	Low	Soup kitchens, clean-up drives
Donations	Low	High	Monthly automated donations
Advocating	Medium	Low	Social media campaigns
Personal Lifestyle Change	Medium	Medium	Recycling, using less plastic
Participating in Events	High	Medium	Attending rallies, fundraising events

Incorporating multiple methods of support can lead to a holistic approach in backing causes you care deeply about. By integrating these practices into our daily lives, we not only help those in need but also grow as individuals who lead by example. Our actions inspire those around us and create a ripple effect, encouraging others to join in and make a difference.

20

COLLABORATIVE MINDSET

"It's amazing what a team can accomplish when you don't care who gets the credit."

~R.A. Dickey

Ever worked on something with a friend and realized that together, you actually made a better team than you expected? This is what a collaborative mindset is all about: working together towards common goals with an open, supportive approach. Instead of just focusing on what each of you is good at, you combine your strengths and fill in for each other's weaknesses. This way, the result is often better than what either of you could have accomplished individually.

When we have a collaborative mindset, we are willing to listen to others' ideas and adjust our own thinking if needed. It means valuing every team member's input and recognizing that everyone has something valuable to contribute. Imagine if every player on a soccer team only cared about scoring goals themselves—they'd miss opportunities to pass the ball or assist someone else in scoring. A winning team works together seamlessly, supporting each other and making decisions that benefit the group instead of just one person.

Working collaboratively also involves sharing resources, whether they're physical materials or skills and knowledge. For example, in the workplace, this might look like one person teaching a colleague how to use a new software tool they're unfamiliar with. The benefits go beyond just the task at hand; it builds trust and encourages an environment where everyone feels comfortable asking for and offering help.

One of the key aspects of developing a collaborative mindset is **self-awareness.** This means understanding your own strengths and weaknesses—and being open about them with your team. If you're good at organizing but not so great at coming up with creative ideas, letting your team know this can create opportunities for others to step in where you're less strong. Likewise, you can take the lead in your areas of expertise.

When promoting collaboration, patience and flexibility are essential. Not every idea will work out perfectly on the first try, and sometimes adapting plans based on feedback will be necessary. But these adjustments often lead to better outcomes in the long run.

TEAMWORK AND COOPERATION

When I think about the times in my life when I've felt the most successful, there's a common thread that runs through all of those moments—teamwork. The journey of life can often feel overwhelming and unpredictable, but having a supportive team can make all the difference. Let's take, for example, a project at work that requires the skills and expertise of multiple people. In such situations, no one person has all the answers. Instead, we rely on our colleagues to bring their unique perspectives and strengths to the table. This is where cooperation comes into play.

I remember being part of a project that was initially daunting. We were tasked with developing a new product within just six months—

a timeline that seemed impossible. But as we came together and started collaborating, each person brought insights and solutions that others hadn't considered. It was like watching puzzle pieces fall into place. One colleague had a knack for market research, another excelled in design, and I lent my skills in project management. By pooling our talents and working together, we not only met our deadline but also created something better than any of us could have achieved alone.

What's essential in teamwork is **clear communication**. Without it, misunderstandings and conflicts can arise, thereby derailing the entire effort. Open lines of communication ensure that everyone is on the same page and working toward a common goal. I find that regular check-ins and updates are valuable tools in maintaining this transparency.

In addition to communication, **mutual respect** is key. A team functions best when each member feels valued and heard. When I respect my teammates' ideas and contributions, it encourages a positive atmosphere where creativity flourishes. It's amazing what we can achieve when we uplift one another.

One particular project comes to mind where mutual respect truly shone through. We were working on an advertising campaign with very tight deadlines. Emotions ran high, but instead of allowing stress to breed negativity, we focused on recognizing each team member's efforts. Rather than pointing fingers when problems arose, we sought solutions together.

Conflict resolution is also an inevitable aspect of teamwork. Differences in opinions are natural; it's how we handle them that counts. I've found that approaching conflicts with an open mind and a willingness to understand others' viewpoints can turn potential roadblocks into opportunities for growth.

Teamwork in Personal Settings

While teamwork is often thought of in professional settings, its principles apply just as strongly in our personal lives. Think about your family or close friends—the bonds you share often require cooperation on a daily basis. Whether it's planning a vacation or deliberating about significant life events, mutual support and making decisions together are crucial.

In friendships too, a collaborative mindset can enhance relationships significantly. I've found that being there for one another during tough times strengthens connections more than anything else.

Visualizing these principles might help cement them further:

PRINCIPLE	ACTIONABLE STEP
Clear Communication	Schedule regular team meetings/check-ins
Mutual Respect	Actively listen and value others' contributions
Conflict Resolution	Address issues openly with an aim to understand

A collaborative mindset isn't limited to achieving tasks but extends to creating environments where everyone thrives both individually and collectively. This reminds me of my experience volunteering for a local community event in organizing resources for families in need during the holidays. The community came together, and everyone understood different aspects—some knew logistics well while others managed outreach or fundraising efficiently. Together, we made it happen successfully!

When I think back on moments like these—whether at work or in everyday life—they remind me of something important: we are not meant to do life alone! Being open to collaboration means welcoming diverse perspectives which not only helps us achieve our goals but also fosters meaningful human connections along the way. The connections we build through teamwork can last a lifetime, influencing and shaping who we are.

Consider another instance where my family decided to host a large reunion. This was no small feat, requiring detailed planning and lots of cooperation. Each member took responsibility for different aspects—one aunt organized the catering, an uncle took care of the venue, while cousins handled decorations and entertainment. By dividing tasks according to strengths, we managed to pull off a memorable event that everyone cherished.

WORKSHEET
Embracing Teamwork and Cooperation

Here's a simple worksheet to help reflect on and incorporate a collaborative mindset:

1. Reflect on Past Experiences: Think of a time when teamwork led to success. Describe the project and how collaboration played a role.

_____

_____

_____

_____

_____

2. Identify Strengths in Your Team: List out skills or strengths of each team member (including yourself) in your current project or situation.

_____

_____

_____

_____

_____

3. Ensure Clear Communication: Plan your next team meeting. What points will you discuss to ensure everyone is on the same page?

_____

_____

_____

_____

_____

4. Promote Mutual Respect: How will you show appreciation for your team members' contributions this week?

_____

_____

_____

_____

_____

5. Handle Conflicts Positively: Describe a potential conflict scenario and how you would approach resolving it with an open mind.

_____

_____

_____

_____

_____

By reflecting on these aspects, we can consistently improve our collaborative efforts, whether at work, with family, or in our communities.

Remember, each individual's input adds value to the collective goal. No one can achieve everything alone; it's through our combined efforts that we find strength, innovation, and success.

SHARING CREDIT AND SUCCESS

With teamwork comes sharing credit and success. One of the most powerful benefits of this is that it **fosters trust and encourages mutual respect.** When we openly acknowledge the contributions of others, it shows that we value their efforts and recognize how their work positively impacts our collective goals.

This not only makes people feel appreciated but also motivates them to continue striving for excellence. Think about it: *wouldn't you be more willing to go the extra mile if you knew your hard work wouldn't go unnoticed?*

Another important aspect of sharing success is that it promotes a **sense of belonging** within a team or community. When everyone feels like they are part of something bigger than themselves, they are more likely to be engaged and committed. It creates an inclusive atmosphere where each member's input is valued, leading to better decision-making and more innovative solutions.

When it comes to the practical side of things, sharing success often means **shared learning opportunities.** When one person or team achieves something noteworthy, there's usually a lesson in there that can benefit others. By highlighting these successes and discussing how they were achieved, we can spread knowledge and best practices throughout the organization or group.

Making it a habit to share credit also helps to **break down silos and encourage cross-functional collaboration**. When people from different departments or backgrounds see that their efforts are being recognized, they're more likely to want to work together on future projects. This kind of synergy can lead to breakthroughs that might not happen if everyone stayed in their own bubbles.

In my experience, the act of sharing credit doesn't diminish your own achievements; in fact, it can enhance your reputation. Leaders who regularly acknowledge their team's contributions are often seen as more genuine and capable because they understand that their success depends on the collective efforts of many, not just their own actions.

Now, let me offer some tips on how you can foster this collaborative mindset and share credit effectively:

1. **Be Observant:** Pay attention to who is contributing what within your team or group. Sometimes the most impactful contributions come from unexpected places.

2. **Speak Up:** Publicly acknowledge the efforts of others when appropriate. Whether it's at meetings or in communications, make it a point to mention who played key roles in successful outcomes.

3. **Write It Down:** Sending thank-you notes or emails recognizing someone's hard work can make a huge difference.

4. **Spread the Word:** Share stories of success across your organization or community through newsletters, social media, or other channels.

5. **Encourage Peer Recognition:** Implement systems where team members can recognize each other's contributions directly.

6. **Lead by Example:** If you're in a leadership position, make sure you set the tone by regularly acknowledging your team's efforts.

Remember, creating an environment where success is shared not only boosts morale but also leads to sustained high performance and innovation over time.

MENTORING AND HELPING OTHERS GROW

Mentoring means that we move from focusing solely on our personal achievements to investing in the success of others. It's a powerful shift that not only uplifts those we mentor but also enriches our own journey.

Mentorship relationships are built on trust, guidance, and mutual respect. As mentors, we pave the path for others to walk with confidence by sharing our knowledge, experiences, and insights. It's about listening actively to their aspirations and challenges, offering tailored advice that resonates with their specific needs.

One of the key aspects of effective mentoring is **empathy**. Putting ourselves in another's shoes allows us to understand their perspectives better. When we relate to their struggles, we're more equipped to provide meaningful support. Empathy also creates a safe space where mentees feel valued and understood, which can significantly enhance their growth trajectory.

Helping others grow isn't confined to formal mentorship programs. It can occur spontaneously in daily interactions at work or in our communities. For instance, when you offer constructive feedback, share resources, or simply be available for a chat, this can create an atmosphere that fosters development.

Let's say you notice a colleague struggling with a presentation. Instead of just offering sympathy, you can take it a step further by providing actionable feedback or suggesting techniques that helped you in the past. This not only helps them with their immediate challenge but also gives them the skills to deal with such situations in the future.

Additionally, I've always found that asking open-ended questions is an effective way of empowering others to find their own solutions. Questions like *"What do you think could be different?"* or *"How might you approach this challenge?"* encourage critical thinking and self-reflection. This way, mentorship evolves from mere advice-giving to nurturing independent problem-solving abilities.

In mentoring relationships, setting clear, well-defined goals makes all the difference. These objectives should be specific, achievable, and time-bound. Whether you are helping someone improve their public speaking skills or master a new software tool, having defined goals provides you with direction and purpose on how to go about it.

Also, make sure you have regular check-ins; they can help you track progress and make any necessary adjustments along the way.

Here's a simple table to lay out how goal-setting can be structured:

GOAL	ACTIONABLE STEP	TIMELINE
Improve Public Speaking	Attend weekly Toastmasters meetings. Practice speaking daily for 10 minutes. Record speeches and review	3 months
Master New Software	Complete an online course. Engage in hands-on exercises	6 weeks

While guiding others on their paths, mentors also experience personal growth. Mentoring sharpens our leadership skills, enhances emotional intelligence, and broadens our perspectives as we learn from diverse experiences of our mentees.

This ripple effect extends beyond individual relationships; it fosters a culture of collaboration within organizations and communities. People become more willing to share knowledge and support each other's development when they experience the benefits firsthand.

This collaborative mindset encourages continual learning, which is an essential component in today's rapidly evolving world. In environments where collective growth is emphasized over individual competition, innovation thrives as people are more likely to experiment and take risks without the fear of failure. Moreover, mentoring helps build strong professional networks rooted in mutual trust and respect. These connections often lead to increased opportunities for career advancement as well as personal fulfillment.

It's important though for mentors to remain open-minded and flexible throughout the process. No two individuals are alike; understanding what works best for each mentee will require your utmost adaptability and patience.

21

BALANCING SELFLESSNESS AND SELF-CARE

"Every one of us needs to show how much we care for each other and, in the process, care for ourselves."

~Princess Diana

In our quest to care for others, we often forget one important element: ourselves. Striking a balance between selflessness and self-care is essential. Why, you ask? Well, as the saying goes, *"You can't pour from an empty cup."* If we're constantly giving without replenishing our own energy and well-being, we risk burnout and resentment.

We need this balance because it allows us to be our best selves for those who depend on us. Think about it: *When you're exhausted or overwhelmed, how effective can you truly be in helping others?* Not very. When we prioritize both self-care and selflessness, we create a sustainable way to keep giving without depleting ourselves.

Finding this balance ensures that we avoid burnout. Constantly giving without also taking time for yourself leads to physical and emotional exhaustion. We start feeling like we have nothing left to give, which can affect every part of our lives—from work to personal relationships.

Also, setting boundaries is easier when you strike that balance. When you're clear about your limits, it's simpler to say "no" when needed without feeling guilty. Boundaries protect your well-being while still allowing you to show up for others in meaningful ways.

Finally, ensuring your personal well-being while helping others is crucial for lasting contributions. It's like being on a long-distance race; pacing yourself ensures you can keep running without falling apart halfway through.

AVOIDING BURNOUT

We've all been there, giving so much of ourselves to others that we end up burned out, wondering where all our energy and joy went. It's super important to strike a balance to keep going strong without losing ourselves in the process.

It's okay to say no. Saying no doesn't mean you're selfish; it means you're human. We often feel pressured to be available for everyone, but constantly putting others first can lead us straight into burnout territory. I had a friend, Jess, who was the go-to person for everything—family issues, work troubles, even neighborhood disputes. She was always helping out because she genuinely cared. But one day she hit a wall; she couldn't give anymore because she was completely drained.

Jess learned the hard way that saying no occasionally is necessary. She started setting boundaries. Not rigid iron walls but reasonable limits on her time and energy. She began to evaluate which commitments were genuinely necessary and which ones she could skip without the world falling apart. And guess what? The world didn't fall apart when she said no once in a while.

Allocating time for yourself isn't just important; it's critical. You need those moments when you're not catering to someone else's needs or solving someone else's problems. Dedicate at least some part of your week solely to activities that recharge you. This could be reading, hiking, painting, or simply enjoying a quiet cup of tea.

Task Prioritization

To make sure you get the important things done without over exhausting yourself, prioritizing tasks is essential. Here, we will use the Eisenhower Box method—it divides tasks into four categories:

1. Urgent and important

2. Important but not urgent

3. Urgent but not important

4. Neither urgent nor important

Here's how it might look in practice:

URGENT & IMPORTANT (DO)	IMPORTANT BUT NOT URGENT (DECIDE)
Family emergency	Doctor's appointments
Work deadlines	Self-care routines
Child's school issues	Exercise routine
URGENT BUT NOT IMPORTANT (DELEGATE)	**NEITHER URGENT NOR IMPORTANT (DELETE)**
Responding to emails	Social media browsing
Answering calls	Watching TV

By categorizing tasks this way, you ensure that your most crucial responsibilities are addressed without neglecting essential self-care routines.

SETTING BOUNDARIES

Think about a time when you felt overwhelmed or stretched too thin. Chances are, you probably struggled to say "no" or found yourself constantly putting others' needs before your own. This is where boundaries come into play. Boundaries are like invisible lines that help protect our well-being and ensure that we can show up as our best selves for both ourselves and others.

Setting boundaries helps us maintain a healthy balance between being there for others and taking care of ourselves. Without boundaries, we're at risk of burnout, resentment, and feeling taken advantage of. Boundaries help us to:

1. **Protect Our Energy:** By setting limits on what we can take on, we conserve our energy for the most important tasks and relationships.

2. **Maintain Mental Health:** Establishing boundaries prevents feelings of overwhelm and stress, promoting better mental health.

3. **Ensure Quality Over Quantity:** When we set boundaries, we prioritize meaningful interactions and activities over constant busyness.

Steps to Setting Effective Boundaries

1. **Identify Your Limits:** Reflect on what you can realistically handle without compromising your well-being. Think about

aspects such as time, emotional energy, physical energy, and personal space.

2. **Communicate Clearly:** Be honest and direct with others about your limits. For example, if you're often asked to stay late at work but need evenings for family time or personal rest, communicate this clearly to your boss or colleagues.

3. **Learn to Say "No":** Saying "no" can be difficult, especially if you're used to being accommodating. Practice assertiveness by politely declining requests that push you beyond your limits.

4. **Use "I" Statements:** Frame your boundaries using "I" statements to express how certain actions affect you personally. For instance, *"I feel overwhelmed when I have too many commitments in one week."*

5. **Be Consistent:** Consistency is key to maintaining boundaries. Stick to your limits even if it feels uncomfortable initially.

6. **Expect Pushback:** Understand that not everyone will be thrilled with your boundaries, especially at the beginning; this is where persistence is even more crucial.

STEP	ACTION	EXAMPLE
1	Identify Your Limits	Determine personal capacity—emotional/physical
2	Communicate Clearly	"I need evenings free for personal time."
3	Learn to Say "No"	Politely decline extra tasks beyond capacity
4	Use "I" Statements	"I feel stressed taking on additional work."
5	Be Consistent	Stick to established limits regularly
6	Expect Pushback	Stay firm even if others react negatively initially

While it might seem counterintuitive, setting boundaries is actually a form of selflessness because it ensures you can give your best when it counts most. By acknowledging and communicating your limits:

- You prevent burnout, which helps sustain long-term support for others.
- You set an example for others to take care of their own needs.
- You foster healthier, more respectful relationships where everyone feels respected and valued.

To put these steps into action, here are a few everyday scenarios:

SCENARIO	SUGGESTED BOUNDARY
Constant work calls after hours	Turn off work phone after 6 PM
Friends dropping by unannounced	Ask friends to call before visiting
Family expecting help on weekends	Reserve weekends for rest, set a specific help slot
Being asked to volunteer frequently	Limit volunteering to certain days/times

ENSURING WELL-BEING WITH SELF-CARE

Striking a balance between selflessness and self-care feels like walking a tightrope. We want to be there for others, but we also need to ensure we're not neglecting our own needs.

Let's discuss ways to maintain this balance across different aspects of our lives.

Physical Well-being

To be at our best for others, we must start with our physical health. As we said, it's impossible to pour from an empty cup, so we need to take care of and nourish our bodies first.

1. Nutrition: Eating balanced meals fuels us throughout the day. I find that having healthy snacks handy makes a big difference when my schedule gets hectic.

2. Exercise: Exercise is another game changer in maintaining balance. Regular physical activity boosts energy levels and reduces stress. You don't need to train for a marathon; even short 30-minute daily walks can have positive effects.

3. Sleep: On the other hand, sleep is often underestimated, yet absolutely vital for keeping burnout at bay. Make sure you're getting quality sleep because it truly does affect everything else. Aim for 7-9 hours per night and establish a calming bedtime routine.

4. Medical Check-ups: Routine health check-ups help catch potential issues early.

Here's a simple chart that I use to keep track of my physical well-being:

Activity	Target Frequency
Balanced Meals	Daily
Exercise	3-5 times per week
Sleep	7-9 hours every night
Health Check-ups	Annually

Mental Well-being

Mental health is just as crucial as physical health. We need strategies to keep our minds sharp and resilient.

1. Mindfulness and Meditation: Practicing mindfulness or meditation helps quiet the mind and reduce stress. This doesn't require hours of your day; even five minutes can make a significant difference. There's compelling evidence supporting the power of mindfulness in reducing stress and improving overall well-being.

2. Learning Something New: Engaging in new activities or hobbies stimulates the brain.

3. Limit Media Consumption: Consuming too much news or social media can be overwhelming, so setting boundaries is key.

4. Seek Support: This could be friends, family, or professionals like therapists or counselors who can provide valuable insights and coping strategies in case of burnout. Remember, there's no shame in consulting a therapist or counselor when things get tough.

Emotional Well-being

Our emotional health determines how we relate to ourselves and others.

1. **Journaling:** Writing down thoughts and feelings can provide clarity and emotional release. A helpful tip is to keep a journal where you jot down patterns indicating you're nearing burnout: feeling overwhelmed frequently, constant irritability, or even physical symptoms like headaches or stomach problems should be red flags signaling the need for immediate adjustments.

2. **Connect with Loved Ones:** Maintaining meaningful relationships is vital for emotional support.

3. **Set Boundaries:** It's essential to know when to say no and protect our emotional energy.

4. **Express Gratitude:** Yes, this simple practice is also vital for self-care, as you acknowledge what you're thankful for each day. This can shift our mindset dramatically toward positivity and make challenges seem more manageable. Start small by noting one thing you're grateful for each day, and you'll notice a gradual shift in your outlook over time.

Spiritual Well-being

Our spiritual health gives us purpose and connects us to something larger than ourselves.

1. **Reflect on Beliefs/Values:** Take time to understand what truly matters to you and why.

2. **Practice Religion/Faith (if applicable):** Engaging in religious or spiritual practices can provide comfort and a sense of community.

3. **Spending Time in Nature:** Connecting with nature can be a powerful way to feel grounded and inspired.

4. **Find Meaningful Activities:** Engage in activities that resonate with your core beliefs, whether this is volunteering, creating art, or participating in community events.

Balancing selflessness with self-care isn't about perfecting each area but finding harmony in our daily lives. By nurturing ourselves, we become better equipped to support others effectively. This balance enables us to show up for life fully—for ourselves and those we care about.

PART VI
FIND PURPOSE

22

THE IMPORTANCE OF PURPOSE

"Believe in your heart that you're meant to live a life full of passion, purpose, magic, and miracles."

~Roy T. Bennett

When I think of purpose, I envision waking up each morning with a clear sense of direction. It's like having a guiding star in the night sky that points you toward what feels right and fulfilling. It helps you steer through life's twists and turns with confidence because you know where you're headed, even if the path isn't always clear.

Having a purpose means having something you're passionate about that drives you. It's not necessarily about just setting goals or achieving success; it's about making your life more meaningful. Purpose is that inner drive that gives direction to your life.

Have you ever noticed how some people just seem to have everything together? They appear happier, healthier, and more focused. It's like they possess some secret ingredient to a fulfilling life. Let me spill the beans - that secret ingredient is a clear sense of purpose.

Think about it this way: When you have a purpose, it's easier to set priorities. Instead of getting bogged down by minor distractions, you stay focused on what really matters to you. This can also make you more resilient. When challenges pop up—and they will—you'll find it easier to push through them because you're driven by something bigger than the obstacles in your way.

Let me share an example from my own life. Some years ago, I was kind of drifting through my days without much direction. I was busy but not fulfilled; I was doing things, but not the things that made my heart sing. Then one day, while volunteering at a local shelter, I discovered my love for helping others find their footing and get back on track with their lives. It was as though a light bulb went off inside me: *This is what I am meant to do!*

From that moment on, everything changed. My actions became aligned with this newfound purpose of helping others. Decisions became easier to make because now they had context; they fit into this bigger picture that gave meaning to my daily grind.

Purpose comes in many forms too—it can be anything from creating art that expresses your deepest thoughts to being the rock for your family through thick and thin, or even working towards social change on a global scale. What matters most is that it resonates deeply with you.

Here's another key point: Your purpose doesn't have to be grand or change the world in obvious ways, though it can be if that's where your passion lies! Often it's about making small differences in the lives around us that collectively lead to a significant impact.

To give you some perspective, let's look at this table:

EVERYDAY ACTIVITY	PURPOSE BEHIND IT
Cooking meals for family	Bringing people together
Painting landscapes	Expressing creativity
Volunteering at animal shelter	Advocating for animal welfare
Starting a small business	Building community connections

Looking at these examples can help illuminate how varied purposes can be, yet how integral they are to making our lives rich and full of meaning.

Remember, discovering your purpose takes time and self-reflection—it's not something you'll necessarily figure out overnight. Sometimes it's hidden in our passions or in the activities that make us lose track of time because we become so engrossed in them.

THE IMPACT OF HAVING A CLEAR SENSE OF PURPOSE

Now let's take a closer look at just how much having a strong sense of purpose can influence our lives, from our physical health to our emotional and mental well-being:

1. Physical Health Benefits: Did you know that having a sense of purpose can actually improve your physical health? Researchers have found that people who feel their lives have meaning tend to live longer.

This means that people with a higher sense of purpose had a much lower risk of dying prematurely compared to those without it. Having a purpose can reduce stress, lower the risk of heart disease, and improve sleep quality.

2. Mental Health Stability: Not only does your physical health benefit from having a defined purpose, but your mental health gets a boost too. Depression and anxiety are more common than we like to admit.

However, people with a strong sense of purpose are often better equipped to handle these mental health challenges. Research showed that individuals with high levels of purpose were less likely to experience symptoms associated with anxiety and depression.

3. Daily Motivation: Imagine waking up every day knowing exactly what you need to do and why you need to do it. That's what having a clear sense of purpose feels like. It's your internal GPS guiding you through life's twists and turns. This level of motivation isn't just good for big life decisions; it also impacts everyday tasks.

Having a purpose can make mundane activities more tolerable or even enjoyable because you understand how they fit into your larger life goals. For instance, if your purpose is related to helping others or improving your community, even small steps toward those goals can feel significant.

4. Enhanced Resilience: Life isn't always smooth sailing; we all face setbacks and obstacles. But as we mentioned, when you have clarity about your purpose, bouncing back from these challenges becomes easier. Purpose acts like an anchor in stormy weather—it keeps you steady amidst turbulence.

It is found that people with purpose are more resilient when faced with adversity compared to those who lack clarity about their "life's direction"

5. Social Connectedness: Humans are social creatures; we thrive on relationships and interactions with others. Having a clear sense of purpose often enhances this aspect too. When you know what drives you, you tend to attract others who share similar values and goals, thereby fostering deeper connections and more meaningful relationships.

Take volunteering as an example—when driven by genuine passion or purpose, it not only provides personal satisfaction but also opens doors to meet like-minded individuals, which amplifies social bonds.

6. Personal Fulfillment: A clear sense of purpose isn't just about achieving external milestones; it's also about internal satisfaction. Feeling that your life has meaning gives you a deeper sense of fulfillment, making everyday experiences richer and more rewarding.

Understanding the various ways a clear sense of purpose impacts our lives—from physical health to social connections—can give you the motivation you need to seek out your purpose.

METHODS TO DISCOVER AND DEFINE YOUR LIFE'S PURPOSE

So, how do you go about figuring out what you're meant to do and what makes you feel alive?

Here are simple steps that can help:

1. Self-Reflection: One of the best ways to start this journey is through self-reflection. Take some quiet time for yourself and think about what truly matters to you. Ask yourself questions like, *"What are my passions?"* and *"What activities make me lose track of time?"* Keep a journal handy to jot down any thoughts or realizations. Example questions for self-reflection:

- What subjects do I enjoy learning about?
- What activities make me feel energized and fulfilled?
- When do I feel at my happiest?

2. Identify Your Strengths: Take stock of your strengths and skills. Knowing what you're good at can help point you in the direction of your life's purpose. You might consider taking a strengths assessment like the CliftonStrengths or VIA Survey (a quick search online can provide more sources).

3. Explore Your Passions: *What are the things you love doing?* Sometimes, our hobbies and interests hold keys to our purpose because they reflect our true selves when we let go of external expectations.

4. Look for Patterns: Review your reflections, strengths, and passions—look for any recurring themes or patterns. These motifs tend to reveal something significant about what you truly value and enjoy in life.

SAMPLE THEMES FROM SELF-DISCOVERY EXERCISES

ACTIVITY/INTEREST	EMOTION FELT	POSSIBLE PURPOSE INDICATOR
Volunteering	Fulfillment	Helping others
Writing	Excitement/joy	Expressing ideas
Teaching kids	Happiness	Educating/mentoring

5. Visualize Your Ideal Future: Spend a few moments visualizing what your ideal life looks like. Think about where you are, who you're with, and what you're doing. Visualization is a powerful tool that helps clarify what feels right for you (refer back to our chapter on visualization for more visualization techniques).

6. Ask for Feedback: Sometimes, others see qualities in us that we don't recognize in ourselves. Ask trusted friends or family members what they think your strengths are or when they've seen you at your best.

7. Examine Your Personal Values: Understanding what values are non-negotiable for you can direct your life's purpose too. *Do values like integrity, freedom, creativity, or kindness resonate deeply with you?* Your answer here gives you a clear picture of how you want to show up in the world.

8. Set Goals That Align with Your Findings: Once you've gathered insights from these different exercises, start setting small goals that align with this newfound sense of purpose. It could be as simple as dedicating an hour each week to something you're passionate about or taking steps toward a new career path.

9. Stay Open to Change: It's essential to remember that discovering your life's purpose isn't a one-time thing; it evolves as we grow and experience new things in life. Stay open to re-evaluating and making adjustments as needed.

If you're finding it challenging to pinpoint your purpose on your own, don't hesitate to seek guidance from a coach or mentor who specializes in personal development. Another excellent method to find your life's purpose is through trial and error. Experiment with different activities or projects that stir your interest and see how they resonate with you. Don't be afraid to step out of your comfort zone; sometimes our purpose is discovered in the most unexpected ways.

WORKSHEET
Identifying Passions And Interests

This worksheet is designed to help you dive deeper into what really excites and fulfills you. Take some time to fill out the sections below:

1. Activities I Enjoy: List at least five activities you love doing.

_____

_____

_____

_____

2. Subjects I Love Learning About: What topics or subjects are you naturally drawn to?

_____

_____

_____

_____

3. Moments I Felt Most Fulfilled: Reflect on past experiences where you felt truly satisfied.

_____

_____

_____

_____

4. Feedback from Others: Ask friends or family members what they think your strengths are and write them down.

PERSON	STRENGTH THEY SEE

5. Values That Resonate with Me: List down values that are very important to you.

_____

_____

_____

_____

_____

6. Patterns and Themes Identified: Looking at all the above sections, note any recurring themes or patterns.

THEME/PATTERN	POSSIBLE PURPOSE INDICATOR

Keep this worksheet handy as it can serve as a reference point for you while navigating through your journey of self-discovery. Remember, finding your purpose is an ongoing journey, not a destination. Stay curious, stay open, and most importantly, stay true to yourself.

When you align your actions with what truly resonates with you, you'll not only feel more fulfilled but also contribute genuinely to the world around you. Keep exploring, keep engaging, and you'll find that the path becomes clearer with each step.

ACTION PLAN
Strategies For Living a Purpose-Driven Life

Living a purpose-driven life is one of the most rewarding experiences one can have—and it's something everyone deserves. By aligning our actions with our true purpose, we not only achieve personal satisfaction but also get the chance to positively impact the lives of others. Here, I'll walk you through an actionable plan to live a purpose-driven life, detailing each step and providing practical strategies to implement them.

1. Define Your Purpose: Based on the previous worksheet, you have probably zeroed in on what your purpose might be. You can write it down below (and as we said, this is subject to change, and that's okay):

My purpose is:

_____

_____

_____

_____

_____

2. Set Goals and Create a Plan: Once you've defined your purpose, the next step is to set clear and achievable goals on how to go about fulfilling your purpose. And as always, break down your main objective into smaller, manageable tasks and make sure these tasks are SMART—Specific, Measurable, Achievable, Relevant, and Time-bound. For example:

GOAL	SPECIFIC TASKS
Start a community garden	Find a location Gather volunteers Seek funding or donations

Creating such detailed plans ensures that you have a roadmap to follow, keeping you motivated and on track.

3. Prioritize Your Time: Time management is crucial when aiming for a purpose-driven life. Identify your key priorities and allocate time accordingly. Avoid time-wasting activities that don't align with your purpose. Use tools like calendars, planners, or apps to keep track of your commitments. Here's an example of how you could allocate time:

- *Morning*: Exercise and meditation
- *Late Morning*: Work on community garden project
- *Afternoon*: Meet with volunteers
- *Evening*: Personal development (reading, learning)

4. Take Action: All the planning in the world won't make a difference if you don't take action. Start executing your plan as soon as possible. It's easy to get caught up waiting for the *"right moment,"* but remember that progress is more important than perfection.

5. Practice Gratitude: When it comes to actualizing your purpose, gratitude is especially important. It will shift your focus from what you lack to what you have, making you more positive about your purpose and life in general. Make it a habit to document things you're grateful for each day—whether it's a supportive friend or achieving a small milestone toward your goal. For example:

Date	POSSIBLE PURPOSE INDICATOR
DD/MM/YY	Thankful for supportive family
DD/MM/YY	Grateful for finding an ideal location for garden

6. Surround Yourself with Positive Influences: Your environment is important in your success. Surround yourself with people who uplift and encourage you rather than those who bring negativity into your life. For instance:

HIGH POSITIVE INFLUENCE	LOW POSITIVE INFLUENCE
Mentors	Negative news channels
Like-minded friends	Naysayers
Inspirational books/podcasts	Toxic relationships

7. Embrace Challenges and Setbacks: Challenges are inevitable when you're pursuing something meaningful. Instead of seeing them as obstacles, view them as opportunities to grow stronger and wiser (we've consistently seen how to do this throughout the book. It's time to apply it here!). Be proactive in seeking solutions rather than dwelling on problems.

8. Embrace Failure as an Opportunity to Learn: Failure should not deter you from continuing your journey; instead, see it as feedback on what doesn't work so you can adjust your strategy accordingly. Reflect on what went wrong and identify lessons learned. Then use these insights to improve future efforts. For example:

FAILURE	LESSONS LEARNED
Low turnout at initial meeting	Need better marketing and outreach strategies
Insufficient funds for project	Explore additional funding avenues or partnerships

9. Celebrate Your Successes: Acknowledging your achievements is crucial for staying motivated. Take time to celebrate both big and small wins along the way. This boosts your morale and reinforces the positive behaviors that got you there. For example:

- Completed first phase of community garden project
- Reached personal fitness goal
- Received positive feedback from volunteers

By integrating these strategies into your life, you'll be well on your way to living a purpose-driven life filled with meaning, joy, and fulfillment. Remember, it's about making consistent progress and staying true to what truly matters to you.

23

CREATING A VISION

"Your vision will become clear only when you can look into your own heart. Who looks outside, dreams; who looks inside, awakes."

~Carl Jung

Besides having a purpose, creating a vision for your life is one of the most empowering steps you can take to show up for life fully. It's like setting a destination for a road trip. Without it, you might end up wandering aimlessly, never quite reaching what truly lights you up. If your purpose is the fire within, your vision is the path it lights up—it gives you a clear, compelling picture of your desired life and guides each decision and action, giving your life direction and meaning.

When you know what you're aiming for, it's easier to stay on track and avoid distractions. Think about it this way: if you tried to build a house without blueprints, it would be chaotic and inefficient. The same goes for your life. Without a vision, it's hard to achieve anything substantial because you don't have a clear picture of what success looks like for you.

Moreover, a personal vision helps you align your daily routines and long-term goals with what truly matters to you. It's about creating harmony between your actions today and your dreams for tomorrow.

This alignment brings satisfaction and fulfillment, making each day meaningful, not just another tick off the calendar.

CRAFTING A PERSONAL MISSION STATEMENT

Why even bother with a personal mission statement? Well, think about this: life can get pretty overwhelming. We have jobs, relationships, hobbies, dreams—we juggle all of these daily. But having a personal mission statement helps in defining what you want out of this mix. It's like having your own life manual that tells you, *"Focus on this!"* or *"This is what truly matters to you."*

To create a meaningful mission statement:

Step 1: Reflect on Your Core Values

Start by thinking deeply about your core values. *What are those essential principles that guide your life? Is it family? Integrity? Passion? Loyalty?* Make a list of at least five values that are non-negotiable for you:

My Core Values:

1. _____
2. _____
3. _____
4. _____
5. _____

Step 2: Identify Your Passions

Next up, reflect on what makes you come alive. *What activities make time fly for you? Is it writing, painting, mentoring others, or solving problems?* Identifying these passions will help ensure that your mission statement is aligned with things you love doing:

My Passions:

1. _____

2. _____

3. _____

Step 3: Consider Your Strengths and Talents

Evaluate what you're naturally good at or the skills you've honed over time. It could be anything from public speaking to empathy or even financial planning. For example:

My Strengths/Talents:

- Public Speaking
- Empathy
- Financial Planning

Step 4: Draft Your Personal Mission Statement

Now comes the fun part! Bring together your core values, passions, and strengths and draft a mission statement that reflects who you are and what you aspire to achieve. Here's a simple template to help:

"I am committed to [Core Values] by [Strengths/Talents] through [Passions/Activities]."

Let me give you an example using my values, passions, and strengths:

"I am committed to family and integrity by using my empathy and public speaking skills through mentoring others."

Feel free to tweak it as much as needed until it resonates perfectly with who you are!

Step 5: Keep It Visible

A mission statement has no power if it's buried in your drawer somewhere! Write it down on sticky notes and plaster them where you'll see them daily—your bathroom mirror, fridge door, workstation.

Step 6: Regularly Revisit and Revise

Your personal mission statement isn't set in stone; as you grow and evolve, so should it! Make it a practice to revisit it every six months or yearly. Here's a quick checklist for reviewing:

- Do my core values still hold true?
- Have my passions shifted?
- Have I developed new strengths?

Having this checklist will ensure that your mission statement stays current and meaningful as you navigate through life's twists and turns.

You might wonder how different areas of our lives fit together seamlessly into our personal mission statement's broad framework. Here's how:

LIFE AREA	GOALS & ACTIVITIES	HOW IT ALIGNS WITH MISSION
Career	Promotion at work	Using strengths like empathy and public speaking to mentor others
Relationships	Spending quality time with family and friends	Reinforcing the value of family and loyalty in everyday interactions
Health	Regular exercise	Staying healthy to be energetic and passionate about my activities
Personal Growth	Learning new skills	Enhancing talents like financial planning for future opportunities
Hobbies	Painting or Writing	Engaging in activities that align with my passion and core values

Aligning each area of your life with your mission statement helps you create a coherent direction that keeps you grounded and focused. This makes it easier to make decisions and prioritize your time effectively. Having this well-thought-out mission statement not only serves as a guide but also keeps you motivated when life's challenges come your way.

SETTING PURPOSE-DRIVEN GOALS

Setting purpose-driven goals involves figuring out the pit stops you need to make along the way. These pit stops, or goals, are what will keep you on track and motivated.

To get started, you'll want to:

- Have a clear idea of your overall vision.
- Once you've got that pinned down, break it down into smaller pieces—these are your goals. Think of them as stepping stones that will help you move closer and closer to your vision.

Purpose-driven goals give meaning and direction to our actions. Without purpose, goals can become tasks we feel obligated to complete rather than steps toward something larger and more fulfilling. Imagine you're passionate about improving your health. Instead of saying, *"I want to lose weight,"* which is pretty broad, you could say, *"I want to lose 10 pounds in three months by eating healthier and exercising."* The second goal has purpose; it's specific and tied directly to something beneficial for your future.

Setting Your Goals: The SMART Way

One common method for setting effective goals is using the SMART criteria. You know: Specific, Measurable, Achievable, Relevant, and Time-bound.

Here's a quick rundown:

1. **Specific:** Clearly define what you want to achieve. Instead of saying "get fit," specify how—like "run three times a week."

2. **Measurable:** Make sure you can track your progress. If your goal is health-related, you might measure this with weekly weigh-ins or tracking your running distance.

3. **Achievable:** Your goal should be challenging but attainable. If you're new to strength training, aiming for a fully sculpted body next month might be too much too soon. Maybe start with lowering your body fat as you work your way up to the muscle.

4. **Relevant:** Ensure the goal matters to you and aligns with other relevant life areas. If family time is important, setting a goal that dramatically reduces that time may not be ideal.

5. **Time-bound:** Set a deadline for achieving the goal to keep yourself accountable. For instance, *"I want to bench press 100 pounds in three months."*

Here's an example of how these elements come together:

General Goal: Get in shape.

SMART Goal: Strength train three times a week (specific) and build up to bench pressing 100 pounds (measurable), which I believe I can achieve (achievable). This helps my overall health (relevant), and I'll reach it within three months (time-bound).

Tracking Progress

Once you've set your SMART goals, it's essential to track your progress. Think of it as checking off milestones on your road map. Use whatever tools work best for you—an app on your phone, a journal, or even a spreadsheet.

Here's a simple template for logging your progress:

Goal	Date	Milestone/Achievement	Notes/Reflection
Bench press 100 pounds in 3 months	Week 1	Bench pressed with the bar	Felt good, could push heavier weights
	Week 2	Added 2.5 pounds	Definitely stronger
Eat healthier	Week 1	All home-cooked meals	Avoided fast food, felt energized
	Week 2	Increased veggie intake	Noticed a positive mood change

Another way to stay on track is by setting mini-goals or checkpoints. These are like smaller pit stops along your journey towards the larger goal.

For our strength training example, a mini-goal could be to do a few reps of unassisted bench presses with the bar. By focusing on these smaller benchmarks, it becomes easier to stay motivated and see progress.

Stay Flexible

Remember, life happens and plans can change. It's important to review your goals regularly and adjust them if needed. Maybe you've found that working out three times a week doesn't fit your schedule, but twice a week does.

Adjust your goal to fit what's realistic and achievable for you now. Flexibility doesn't mean giving up; it means recognizing that growth is a dynamic process.

Create an Accountability System

Having someone to share your goals with can also be incredibly helpful. Whether it's a friend, family member, or coach, having someone check in on your progress adds an extra layer of accountability.

You could also join a group with similar objectives, like a local gym or an online community focused on weight lifting.

Reflect and Reassess

Finally, take time to reflect on your journey. *What worked? What didn't?* Use this reflection to tweak future goals and improve your strategy. Don't forget to celebrate your achievements, no matter how small they might seem. Each step forward is progress, and acknowledging these wins helps keep you motivated.

By following these steps, you'll find yourself better equipped to achieve what you set out to do. Remember, each goal achieved is a step closer to fulfilling your purpose-driven vision.

VISUALIZING YOUR FUTURE

I find it essential to visualize my future. It's not about seeing an exact picture of every detail, but more about understanding what I want my life to feel and look like. Let's discuss how you can create a powerful vision for your future. Grab a notebook or open a blank document on your computer. Find a quiet space where you won't be disturbed for a while. This is your time to dream big without any limitations (feel free to use the visualization techniques we learned about earlier).

Let's start by asking ourselves some fundamental questions:

1. *Where do I want to be in 5, 10, or even 20 years?* Think about the different aspects of your life: career, relationships, health, personal development, and leisure. Picture yourself in the future and describe what success looks like for each of these areas. Paint a vivid picture with as many details as possible.

2. *What values are most important to me?* Values are guiding principles that shape our actions and decisions. Identifying your core values will ensure that your vision aligns with what truly matters to you. Write down at least five values that resonate with you deeply.

3. *Who inspires me and why?* Think about people whose lives or achievements you admire. What qualities do they have that you aspire to? How can you incorporate these qualities into your own life?

Next, let's create a vision board. A vision board is a visual representation of your goals and dreams. It could be a physical board with cut-out images from magazines or an online version using tools like Pinterest or Canva. Steps to create your vision board:

1. **Gather Materials:** Get some magazines, scissors, glue, and a board if you're making a physical one. For the online version, choose your platform of choice and select a board that appeals to you.

2. **Find Images and Words:** Look for pictures and words that represent your goals and dreams. For online, you can download/screenshot a few pictures of this.

3. **Arrange Them On The Board**: Place them in a way that feels right to you.

4. **Keep it Visible:** Put your vision board somewhere you'll see it often. For the physical version, you can have it on your fridge or near your working station; for the online version, you can use it as your desktop or phone background.

Creating this visual reminder will help keep your goals at the forefront of your mind and inspire you every day. Remember that creating a vision for your future not only gives you direction but also empowers you to live each day with purpose. Start today by visualizing the kind of life you want to lead and taking tangible steps towards making that vision a reality.

24

INSPIRING OTHERS WITH YOUR PURPOSE

"Purpose spurs passion which fans the sparks that light the fires that fuel change."

~Sir Richard Branson

When you know your purpose and you show up every day to live it, something incredible happens. You start to inspire those around you. It might surprise you how much your actions and dedication can influence others, but it's true—people watch what you do and often take note more than you realize. I want to share with you some key points on how demonstrating your purpose can help inspire those around you in lasting, meaningful ways.

1. Push Through

One of the most powerful ways to inspire others is through perseverance. When others see you pushing through challenges, staying true to your mission even when the going gets tough, they start to believe that they can do it too. Living with purpose isn't just about the good days; it's about how you handle the setbacks and struggles as well. Remember, it's during these times that your commitment to your purpose will shine the brightest.

2. Be Open

I've found that sharing your journey openly and honestly is another great way to inspire others. We all love a good story, and real-life narratives are incredibly impactful. Talk about where you started, the steps you've taken along the way, and where you hope to go in the future. Sharing both your successes and failures makes your journey relatable and authentic, which can be very motivating for others.

Here's an example—think of a time when someone shared their struggles with you and how they overcame them. *Didn't it feel like a breath of fresh air?* That's what sharing your journey can do for someone else. It's powerful when people see that someone who has succeeded was once in their shoes—facing similar doubts and fears.

3. Engage

Actively involving others in your mission is another great way to inspire them. Whether it's inviting someone to join a project you're passionate about or seeking advice from someone who has a different perspective, making people part of your journey creates collective energy that's incredibly motivating.

You're not just telling them about your purpose; you're giving them a chance to be part of it.

4. Encourage

Encouragement also plays a huge role in inspiring others. Often, people need just a little boost or acknowledgment to feel better equipped to pursue their own goals. A simple word of appreciation or a nod of encouragement when someone takes a step towards their own purpose can make a profound difference. Never underestimate the power of small gestures; they can have ripple effects far beyond what you might expect.

5. Lead by Example

This is foundational when it comes to inspiring others with your purpose. Nothing speaks louder than actions aligned with words. Consistently demonstrating commitment, passion, and integrity in what we do shows others that it's not only possible but also rewarding to live with purpose.

6. Little Things Make A Big Difference

And sometimes, it's the little things that make the biggest impact—showing up on time, keeping promises, treating everyone with kindness and respect—these actions build trust and show reliability. When people see these qualities in someone committed to their purpose, they're more likely to feel inspired to incorporate similar practices into their own lives.

7. As Always, Be Optimistic

Maintaining a positive attitude can significantly influence those around us as well. As we established, optimism is contagious; when we approach our purpose-driven journey with enthusiasm and positivity despite any hurdles we face, it lifts others' spirits too.

In short, living out our purpose has this magical ability to light up not just our path but also the paths of those around us. When they see us striving towards something meaningful with resilience and integrity, they're reminded that they too have within them what it takes to pursue their dreams.

KEY ACTIONS	IMPACT
Perseverance in challenges	Demonstrates strength and builds belief
Sharing journey openly	Makes mission relatable
Involving others in your mission	Creates collective energy and motivation
Offering encouragement	Boosts others' confidence and morale
Leading by example	Builds trust and shows reliability
Maintaining a positive attitude	Spreads optimism and lifts spirits

By staying true to these principles, you not only make strides in your own journey but also become a beacon of inspiration for those around you. Remember, it's often the consistent, everyday actions born out of living your purpose that leave the most lasting impact.

THE LEGACY OF A PURPOSEFUL LIFE

Indeed, living a purposeful life impacts us, those around us and our future generations as well. It's fascinating how living with intention and aiming to leave a positive mark can define our legacy.

I've seen how people who have clear goals and purposes in life tend to leave behind lasting memories and contributions that resonate beyond their own lifetime. For instance, consider historical figures like Martin Luther King Jr. or Mother Teresa. Their lives were driven by strong, clear purposes and their legacies are etched in history.

This is what they did and the impact it left:

PERSON	PURPOSE	LEGACY
Martin Luther King Jr.	Civil Rights Activism	Inspirational speeches, pivotal role in the Civil Rights Movement
Mother Teresa	Helping the Poor	Founded Missionaries of Charity, Nobel Peace Prize

But it's not just these monumental achievements that count. Small acts of kindness, consistency in showing up for your commitments, and positively influencing your immediate circles hold immense value too.

I remember my grandmother, who wasn't famous or held any large public office but her dedication was inspirational. She showed up every day with such love and determination to make her family's life better. We talk often about the stories she shared, her values, and even simple recipes that have become a family tradition now. Her legacy of nurturing love and persistence is still very much alive within our family.

Nowadays, even the smallest actions can go viral or inspire others globally. Think of the numerous influencers or bloggers who started simply by sharing their passion or knowledge about something they truly cared about. Over time, they've built communities around those passions by continually showing up for their audience.

But this doesn't mean you need to have your life's purpose figured out right from the start—many find it through experiences over time. What's crucial is taking proactive steps towards discovering what drives you personally.

For me, finding purpose meant trying various paths before realizing my passion for writing and connecting with people through stories. Each attempt wasn't a trial but rather a step closer to understanding myself better.

Therefore, while it's incredibly inspiring to look at accomplished leaders or historical figures as examples, it's important to remember that they all started somewhere simple too—with a desire to create meaning in their own lives first before impacting others. The same goes for you. Your daily decisions, be it at work, home, or amongst friends, reflect your values. These greatly contribute to the impact you have on others and to building your legacy over time.

ENCOURAGING OTHERS TO FIND THEIR PURPOSE

When I think back on my own journey of discovering my purpose, I realize it wasn't something that just happened overnight. The path was filled with trial and error, moments of doubt, and significant breakthroughs. Everyone's journey towards finding their purpose is unique, but one thing remains universal—we all need encouragement along the way.

That's why it's so crucial to encourage others to find their purpose. It's a way to show up not just for yourself but for those you care about. Here are some steps that can help in encouraging others on their journey.

1. Be a Listener: One of the most powerful tools you have is your ability to listen. Sometimes, someone just needs a sounding board to articulate their thoughts or understand their feelings better. Pay attention without interrupting and offer feedback only when asked. Your empathetic listening can help them sort out what's meaningful to them.

2. Share Personal Experiences: Don't be afraid to share your own journey towards finding your purpose. Sharing your highs and lows can provide valuable insights and reassure them that it's okay to stumble along the way. Real-life examples can illustrate points more vividly than abstract words ever could.

3. Ask Guiding Questions: Instead of telling someone what their purpose should be, guide them with thoughtful questions. Consider asking the same questions you asked yourself when defining your purpose:

- What activities make you lose track of time?
- What issues or causes are you passionate about?
- When do you feel most fulfilled?

These questions help spark self-reflection and can lead them to discover what truly matters to them.

4. Encourage Small Steps: Finding one's purpose can feel overwhelming if viewed as a giant leap from where they are now. Encourage taking small, actionable steps instead of giant leaps. Suggest starting with something manageable that aligns with what they care about deeply.

STEP	EXAMPLE ACTION
1	Volunteer for a cause they're passionate about
2	Take up a hobby related to their interest
3	Attend workshops or seminars

Taking baby steps builds confidence and clarifies what feels right.

5. Celebrate Their Progress: If it's someone you are close to, honor and celebrate even the smallest achievements they make along their journey. Recognize when they've made a tough decision or taken a brave step toward what makes them happy. Celebrating progress invigorates motivation and reinforces positivity.

6. Offer Resources: Sometimes people don't know where to start looking for direction or inspiration. Share books, articles, podcasts, and documentaries that have helped you or others in similar situations find clarity or motivation.

7. Create a Supportive Environment: Encouragement flourishes in an uplifting environment. Be that positive influence who exudes hope and possibilities rather than doubts and negativity. Surrounding someone with positivity can empower them faster than you'd think.

8. Be Patient: Lastly, be patient. Remember that finding one's purpose is a journey, not a destination, and it often takes time and introspection. Your role as a supporter is to provide consistent encouragement without pushing too hard or rushing the process. Understand that they will face setbacks and moments of doubt—these are natural and crucial parts of the journey.

And as you know, searching for one's purpose can be emotionally taxing; remind them of the importance of self-care throughout this introspective process. Encourage taking time off if they feel overwhelmed and remind them it's okay not to have all the answers immediately.

It's important to recognize that each person's path to discovering their purpose is unique. What works for one individual might not work for another. Celebrate their individuality by acknowledging their unique strengths, interests, and experiences. This validation can give them the confidence they need to pursue their own path.

Incorporating these strategies into your interactions with others seeking their purpose provides invaluable support that can make all the difference in their journey. Remember, showing up for others is one of the most meaningful ways you can contribute to their growth and fulfillment.

Finding one's purpose is a process—sometimes a slow-moving one—and it's essential to be patient with yourself as well when you're encouraging someone else.

CONTINUOUS PURSUIT OF PURPOSE

Over the years, I've come to realize that finding one's purpose isn't a one-time event; it's a continuous journey. As we grow and evolve, so too does our understanding of why we are here and what we are meant to do. It's like tending to a garden. Initially, you plant seeds with care and attention, but as seasons change, so does the garden. You'll need to water it regularly, pull out weeds, and sometimes replant certain areas to maintain its beauty and efficiency.

One key element I've found essential in my continuous pursuit of purpose is reflection. Taking time to assess where I am in life and understanding how my experiences shape my evolution helps keep me on track. Whether it's journaling at the end of each week or taking a moment during a long walk to contemplate life's bigger picture, these small habits can provide immense clarity.

Another important aspect is flexibility. Life is unpredictable and often throws curveballs when least expected. Embracing change rather than resisting it has allowed me to adapt my sense of purpose without feeling lost or overwhelmed. Think about purpose as a compass rather than a map. While maps provide a specific route, a compass points you in the right direction and allows for course corrections as needed.

There's an exercise I like to do periodically that helps me recalibrate my compass. I hope it will help you:

1. Current Passions: List out your current interests or things that excite you. Evaluate how they align with your activities or career.

a. _____

b. _____

c. _____

d. _____

e. _____

f. _____

2. Strengths and Skills: Note down your key strengths. Determine how effectively you're utilizing them.

a. _____

b. _____

c. _____

d. _____

e. _____

f. _____

3. Goals and Dreams: Write down both short-term and long-term goals. Assess if your current path brings you closer to these dreams.

SHORT-TERM GOALS	LONG-TERM GOALS

Does your current path align with both?

___
___
___
___
___
___
___

EXAMPLE PURPOSE REFLECTION CHART

ASPECT	CURRENT STATUS	ADJUSTMENT NEEDED
Passions	Writing articles on mental health	Dedicate more time weekly
Strengths	Excellent communicator	Leverage this for public speaking
Short-Term Goal	Publish 2 articles a month	Create a writing schedule
Long-Term Dream	Author a book	Plan book concept and outline

This simple exercise can be incredibly eye-opening. It makes you aware of areas in your life that might need adjustment in order to align more closely with your ever-evolving sense of purpose.

Mentorship is also important in the continuous pursuit of purpose. By engaging with mentors and peers who challenge us intellectually and emotionally, we gain new perspectives that can lead us closer to our goals. Sometimes, an outside viewpoint is what's needed to see things from another angle or inspire renewed passion.

Remember, your network serves as an invaluable resource not just for professional growth but for personal satisfaction too. Discussing your ambitions and fears openly with trusted individuals can provide both reassurance and valuable insights.

I encourage you to remain curious—never lose your zest for learning new things or exploring uncharted territories within your capabilities. Curiosity prevents stagnation, leading us towards paths we might have never considered otherwise.

Finally, I want to underline the importance of self-compassion on this journey toward purpose. It's easy to be hard on ourselves when we feel like we're not progressing or when we face setbacks. But remember, every step—no matter how small—is meaningful. Be kind to yourself and acknowledge your efforts.

It's crucial to strike a balance between striving for your goals and being patient with yourself during the process. The continuous pursuit of purpose should be an enriching experience, one that nourishes your soul and brings you closer to understanding yourself better.

Keep moving forward with intention, always keep your compass handy, and remember—you are exactly where you need to be on this journey towards purpose.

CONCLUSION
FOLLOWING THE SHOW UP ROAD MAP

As we come to the end of our journey together in *"SHOW UP For Life: A Personal Road Map for Navigating the Journey"*, I hope you're inspired and motivated to incorporate the SHOW UP characteristics into your daily life. Let's recap these essential traits and quickly review practical strategies for integrating each of them into our routines. Before that, just take a moment to appreciate how far you've come!

BE SELF-AWARE

Self-awareness is the foundation of all personal development. Understanding who you are, recognizing your strengths, weaknesses, emotions, and thoughts allows you to navigate life more effectively. To integrate it into your everyday life, do:

   a. *Daily Self-Reflection:* Spend 10 minutes before bed journaling your thoughts and feelings. This simple exercise can reveal patterns and insights.

   b. *SWOT Analysis Quarterly:* Assess your Strengths, Weaknesses, Opportunities, and Threats every three months. This keeps you on track and aware of your growth areas.

c. *Mindfulness Practices:* Incorporate short mindfulness exercises throughout your day. Use triggers like waiting for the microwave or sitting in traffic to center yourself in the present moment.

d. *Emotional Check-ins:* Set reminders to pause and identify what you're feeling at several points during the day. This builds emotional intelligence over time.

HAVE A SENSE OF HUMOR

Humor is a powerful tool that enhances well-being, strengthens relationships, and helps us navigate difficult times with grace. Here's how to integrate it daily:

a. *Laughter Breaks:* Watch a short, funny video or read a joke before starting work to create a pleasant mood.

b. *Humor Journaling:* Note down funny incidents or humorous thoughts at the end of each day. Reflect on these moments when you need a pick-me-up.

c. *Playful Interactions:* Find safe ways to incorporate humor into conversations with family, friends, and colleagues. Light-hearted banter can strengthen bonds.

BE OPTIMISTIC

Optimism opens doors to happiness and success by fostering a positive mindset that looks for opportunities in challenges. For daily integration:

a. *Gratitude Lists:* Every morning, jot down three things you're grateful for. This practice shifts focus toward positive aspects of life.

b. *Visualization Techniques:* Spend a few minutes each day visualizing positive outcomes and setting clear goals.

c. *Optimistic Inner Dialogue:* Challenge negative thoughts by consciously reframing them into positive statements.

SHOW WARMTH

Warmth fosters genuine connections and creates environments where people feel valued and supported. To integrate daily:

a. *Active Listening Practice:* During conversations, focus fully on the speaker without planning your response. Reflect back what they've said to show understanding.

b. *Small Acts of Kindness Daily:* Hold open doors, smile at strangers, or leave positive notes for loved ones. These small gestures can make a significant impact.

c. *Warm Environment Creation:* Make spaces inviting by adding personal touches like photos or pleasant scents.

BE UNSELFISH

Being unselfish involves considering others' needs alongside our own and contributing generously to their well-being. To integrate daily:

a. *Volunteer Regularly:* Dedicate time weekly or monthly to volunteer at local organizations. Giving back is fulfilling and builds community spirit.

b. *Practice Generosity Daily:* Offer help without being asked or share resources with those in need within your capacity.

c. *Balanced Self-care Planning:* Ensure you set boundaries to manage giving without depleting yourself—don't forget to schedule 'me-time' as part of your routine.

FIND PURPOSE

Purpose adds meaning to our lives, guiding our decisions and providing a sense of direction and fulfillment. To integrate daily:

a. *Reflect on Passions and Interests:* Take time to explore what genuinely excites and interests you. This can be done through journaling, talking to trusted friends, or engaging in new activities to discover hidden passions.

b. *Set Clear Intentions:* Begin each day with a clear intention. Ask yourself what you want to achieve and how it aligns with your broader purpose.

c. *Create a Vision Board:* Visual representations of your goals and dreams can keep your purpose front and center in your life.

d. *Regularly Reevaluate Your Goals:* As we grow and change, so may our purpose. Check in with yourself periodically to ensure your actions still align with your evolving sense of purpose.

As you reflect on everything we've covered—from self-awareness to finding your purpose—remember that this road map is designed to be both a guide and a lifelong companion. Review it as many times as you need to and evolve with it.

Understanding yourself better, finding humor in daily life, maintaining an optimistic outlook, showing warmth to others, being unselfish, and discovering your purpose are not just principles—these are life strategies that will empower you to live fully and authentically. They'll enable you to SHOW UP for life.

REFLECTIVE EXERCISES FOR ONGOING PROGRESS

To ensure you continue making progress, I've included some reflective exercises below. Take your time with these exercises. Use them as checkpoints to assess how well you're integrating the SHOW UP principles into your life.

1. Self-Awareness Checkpoint: Reflect on your current level of self-awareness.

a. What new insights have you gained about yourself?

_____

_____

_____

b. Have you been able to identify and leverage your strengths while addressing your weaknesses?

_____

_____

_____

2. Sense of Humor Evaluation:

a. How often do you find humor in everyday situations?

_____
_____
_____
_____

b. Have you noticed any positive changes in your social interactions due to humor? If yes, how?

_____
_____
_____
_____

3. Optimism Gauge:

a. Are you practicing gratitude regularly? How often?

_____
_____
_____
_____

b. Have you seen improvements in your overall mood and outlook on life?

_____
_____
_____
_____

4. Warmth and Connection Review:

a. How have small acts of kindness impacted your relationships?

_____
_____
_____
_____

b. How are you actively listening and showing empathy towards others?

_____
_____
_____
_____
_____

5. Unselfish Behavior Audit: Reflect on recent unselfish acts you've performed.

a. Are you finding a balance between being unselfish and taking care of yourself? How?

_____
_____
_____
_____

b. If you answered yes to the above question, what are the benefits of finding this balance?

_____
_____
_____
_____

6. Purpose Alignment Assessment:

a. How clear is your sense of purpose?

_____
_____
_____
_____

b. Are you living in alignment with what truly matters to you?

_____

_____

_____

_____

ENCOURAGEMENT TO CONTINUE SHOWING UP

I want to encourage you to keep showing up for yourself and others every single day. Life's journey is filled with ups and downs, opportunities and challenges, moments of joy and periods of sorrow. Through it all, remember the power of showing up.

SHOW UP for your goals, even when they seem out of reach.

SHOW UP for your relationships, even when it feels challenging.

SHOW UP for yourself by practicing self-care and self-compassion.

The journey doesn't end here; it evolves as you grow and learn. Take all that you've learned from this book and apply it daily. Revisit these chapters whenever you need a refresher or some motivation. Your commitment to personal growth not only enriches your life but also has a ripple effect on those around you.

Keep showing up because the world needs more people like you who are dedicated to making a difference by living authentically, spreading kindness, nurturing optimism, fostering connections, practicing unselfishness, and pursuing true purpose.

Here's to navigating the journey with confidence, resilience, and joy!

SUGGESTED READINGS

1. Bariso, Justin (2018). *EQ Applied: The Real-World Guide to Emotional Intelligence.* Borough Hall.

2. Bradberry, T., & Greaves, J. (2009). Emotional Intelligence 2.0. TalentSmart.

3. Brown, B. (2022). *The gifts of imperfection: Let go of who you think you're supposed to be and embrace who you are.* Simon and Schuster.

4. Cardaciotto, L., Herbert, J. D., Forman, E. M., Moitra, E., & Farrow, V. (2008). The assessment of present-moment awareness and acceptance: The Philadelphia Mindfulness Scale. *Assessment*, 15(2), 204–223. https://doi.org/10.1177/1073191107311467

5. Conversano C., Rotondo A., Lensi E., Della Vista O., Arpone F., Reda MA. Optimism and its impact on mental and physical well-being. *Clinical Practice & Epidemiology in Mental Health.* 2010 May 14;6:25-9. doi: 10.2174/1745017901006010025. PMID: 20592964; PMCID: PMC2894461.

6. Fox, J. (2021, December 17). Journaling for Self-Discovery: How to Start. Retrieved from https://feelmoreconnected.com/journaling-for-self-discovery/

7. Frankl, V. E. (2018). *Man's search for ultimate meaning.* Hachette UK.

8. Goldsmith, Marshall and Mark Reiter (2015). Triggers: *Creating Behavior That Last—Becoming the Person You want to Be.* Crown Business.

9. How to develop an attitude of gratitude—Diversus Health. (n.d.). Retrieved from https://diversushealth.org/mental-health-blog/how-to-develop-an-attitude-of-gratitude/

10. Johnson, A. (2019). *Coaching Made Easy: A Framework for Enhancing Performance.* OASYS Press.

11. Kim ES, Chen Y, Nakamura JS, Ryff CD, VanderWeele TJ. Sense of Purpose in Life and Subsequent Physical, Behavioral, and Psychosocial Health: An Outcome-Wide Approach. *American Journal of Health Promotion.* 2022 Jan;36(1):137-147. doi: 10.1177/08901171211038545. Epub 2021 Aug 18. PMID: 34405718; PMCID: PMC8669210.

12. Owasi, D. (2020, June 2). Emotional awareness: recognizing your emotions and their effects. Retrieved from https://www.linkedin.com/pulse/emotional-awareness-recognizing-your-emotions-effects-david-owasi

13. Park SQ, Kahnt T, Dogan A, Strang S, Fehr E, Tobler PN. A neural link between generosity and happiness. Nat Commun. 2017 Jul 11;8:15964. doi: 10.1038/ncomms15964. PMID: 28696410; PMCID: PMC5508200.

14. Positive thinking: Stop negative self-talk to reduce stress. (2023, November 21). Retrieved from https://www.mayoclinic.org/healthy-lifestyle/stress-management/in-depth/positive-thinking/art-20043950

15. Personal SWOT Analysis: How to Conduct One (With Examples). (n.d.). Retrieved from https://www.betterup.com/blog/personal-swot-analysis

16. Reid, S. (2024, June 24). Empathy: how to feel and respond to the emotions of others. Retrieved from https://www.helpguide.org/articles/relationships-communication/empathy.htm

17. Robinson, L., Smith, M., MA, & Segal, J., PhD. (2024, February 5). Laughter is the Best Medicine - HelpGuide.org. Retrieved from https://www.helpguide.org/articles/mental-health/laughter-is-the-best-medicine.htm

18. Self-Reflection: What does it mean & how to Self-Reflect. (n.d.). Retrieved from https://www.betterup.com/blog/self-reflection

19. Sun X, Zhang J, Wang Y, Zhang X, Li S, Qu Z, Zhang H. The impact of humor therapy on people suffering from depression or anxiety: An integrative literature review. Brain Behav. 2023 Sep;13(9):e3108. doi: 10.1002/brb3.3108. Epub 2023 Jun 21. PMID: 37340873; PMCID: PMC10498079.

20. 12 practical tips for living a purpose-driven life. (n.d.). Retrieved from https://www.corepurpose.co.nz/blog/living_a_purpose-driven_life

ABOUT THE AUTHOR

Alonzo Johnson, Ph.D., is a certified life coach and author of the *Made Easy Series*, featuring book titles: *Coaching Made Easy*, *Leading Made Easy,* and *Hiring Made Easy as PIE*. Alonzo is passionate about helping people grow professionally and fulfills this passion by coaching others, while serving as Managing Partner of The OASYS Group, a talent management consulting company focused on helping organizations to effectively manage talent and performance.

With over three decades of experience and leadership skills gained from the military, higher education, and private business sector, Alonzo specializes in coaching leaders to improve their effectiveness by leveraging assessments to foster greater awareness of self. Alonzo has been successful in using self-awareness as a catalyst for meaningful exploration towards personal and professional growth for his clients. He is the developer of the ***LEAD 360° and COACH^{180} assessments***, and is certified to administer and interpret the results of various assessments, including the **EQ-i 2.0®, Benchmarks®, Skillscope®, FIRO Element B™**, and **ARSENAL™**. Alonzo applies a variety of coaching techniques to guide clients to personal and professional fulfillment.

www.ingramcontent.com/pod-product-compliance
Lightning Source LLC
Chambersburg PA
CBHW062242300426
44110CB00034B/1174